Legend

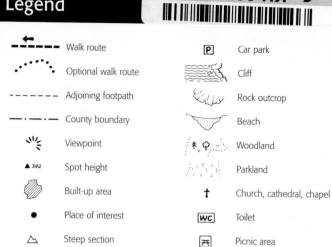

← ——	Walk route	P	Car park
•••••	Optional walk route		Cliff
— — —	Adjoining footpath		Rock outcrop
—·—·—	County boundary		Beach
☀	Viewpoint	♠ ♣	Woodland
▲ 392	Spot height		Parkland
	Built-up area	†	Church, cathedral, chapel
●	Place of interest	WC	Toilet
△	Steep section	🎪	Picnic area

Worcestershire & Herefordshire locator map

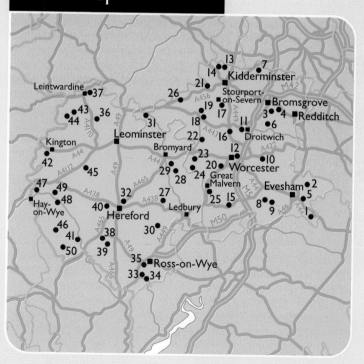

Contents

Contents

Rating: Each walk is rated for its relative difficulty compared to the other walks in this book. Walks marked 🚶 🚶 🚶 are likely to be shorter and easier with little total ascent. The hardest walks are marked 🚶 🚶 🚶 .

Walking in Safety: For advice and safety tips ➤ 128.

Introducing Worcestershire & Herefordshire

Worcestershire is a county of generally rolling hills, save for the flat and fruity Vale of Evesham in the east and the prominent spine of the Malverns in the west. Nearly all of the land is worked in some way; arable farming predominates – oilseed rape, cereals and potatoes – but there are concentrated areas of specific land uses, such as market gardening and plum growing. The county is not without surprises – in Stourport it has Britain's only town created because of a new canal; it has Droitwich Spa, a former site of inland salt production; and its long distance footpath, the Worcestershire Way, has some fine 'ridge' sections, at Rodge Hill (► Walk 22) in particular.

In Herefordshire the land is hillier, abutting in the west with the Black Mountains ridge that defines the border with Wales. Crops are important here, but there are more green fields – for grazing, silage or hay – because this is livestock country; you may be surprised by the large number of sheep, since the 'Hereford' breed of cattle has acquired such fame. And you can't walk for long in this county without seeing an apple orchard.

There are short walks around each county's capital. In the city of Worcester (► Walk 12), which is by far the larger of the two, parts of the core have been reasonably well held on to, New Street, in particular, and Worcester's Commandery (museum) is a regular crowd-puller. The city of Hereford (► Walks 32 and 40) essentially escaped wartime bombing but suffered considerable damage from sorties made by trendy architects in the 1960s (and subsequently), but the cathedral area and the riverside – Castle Green and Bishops Meadow – have retained, thus far, their charm.

The two counties offer plenty of other 'things to do'. My highlights would include some time on a river, the view from Hereford Cathedral's tower, watching a horse working the cider mill at Shortwood Farm (near Pencombe), and eating too many plums in the Vale of Evesham.

In these pages you will find much evidence of past activity: there are churches, castles and mansions (some in use, some in ruins), railways (disappearing and disappeared), canals (extant and extinct) and a pot-pourri of personalities.

PUBLIC TRANSPORT ⓘ

The three linear walks in this book are Walks 21, 25 and 40, using train, train and bus, respectively. (It's always better to take your car to the end and use public transport back to the beginning.) Of the other 47 there are frankly few where you could reach the start by public transport if, say, staying here on holiday. The urban centres are the focus of bus service provision; for a village to have a bus service may mean no more than a bus into town on market day morning, returning in the afternoon.

I've made no conscious effort to select routes beside rivers, yet there are several. Perhaps they hold a subliminal attraction, or is it just that their abundance makes them hard to avoid? They include the rivers Severn, Wye, Avon, Teme and Frome, to name just five. And, in Herefordshire's Golden Valley (➤ Walks 41 and 48/49) 'Dore' is the name of the river that runs through it. The name possibly arises from a confusion of languages. The Welsh referred to the valley's river as dwr, meaning 'water', and some think that the Normans mistook this for d'or, the French for 'of gold' – it was an appropriate mistake to make! Vagar Hill, on the north side of the Golden Valley, is threatened with wind farms, a mind-bogglingly intrusive idea which could diminish that part of the county as a tourist destination. You'd better hurry up and do those walks, just in case.

If it's coastal walking you want, then you've come to the wrong place, but otherwise you're sure to find something to delight you in Worcestershire and Herefordshire.

Using this Book

Information panels

An information panel for each walk shows its relative difficulty (➤ 5), the distance and total amount of ascent. An indication of the gradients you will encounter is shown by the rating 🔺🔺🔺 (no steep slopes) to 🔺🔺🔺 (several very steep slopes).

Maps

There are 30 maps, covering 40 of the walks. Some walks have a suggested option in the same area. The information panel for these walks will tell you how much extra walking is involved. On short-cut suggestions the panel will tell you the total distance if you set out from the start of the main walk. Where an option returns to the same point on the main walk, just the distance of the loop is given. Where an option leaves the main walk at one point and returns to it at another, then the distance shown is for the whole walk. The minimum time suggested is for reasonably fit walkers and doesn't allow for stops. Each walk has a suggested map. Laminated aqua3 maps are longer lasting and water resistant.

Start Points

The start of each walk is given as a six-figure grid reference prefixed by two letters indicating which 100km square of the National Grid it refers to. You'll find more information on grid references on most Ordnance Survey maps.

Dogs

We have tried to give dog owners useful advice about how dog friendly each walk is. Please respect other countryside users. Keep your dog under control, especially around livestock, and obey local bylaws and other dog control notices.

Car Parking

Many of the car parks suggested are public, but occasionally you may find you have to park on the roadside or in a lay-by. Please be considerate when you leave your car, ensuring that access roads or gates are not blocked and that other vehicles can pass safely. Remember that pub car parks are private and should not be used unless you have the owner's permission.

Walk 1

William Morris's Broadway

A haunt of the Arts and Crafts pioneer towers above this Worcestershire village.

•DISTANCE•	5 miles (8km)
•MINIMUM TIME•	2hrs 30min
•ASCENT / GRADIENT•	755ft (230m) ▲▲ ▲ ▲
•LEVEL OF DIFFICULTY•	🚶🚶 🚶🚶 🚶
•PATHS•	Pasture, rough, tree-root path, pavements, 8 stiles
•LANDSCAPE•	Flat vale rising to escarpment
•SUGGESTED MAP•	aqua3 OS Explorer OL45 The Cotswolds
•START / FINISH•	Grid reference: SP 094374
•DOG FRIENDLINESS•	Sheep-grazing country (some cattle and horses too) so only off lead in empty fields; some stiles may be tricky
•PARKING•	Pay-and-display, short stay, 4hrs maximum in Church Close, Broadway; longer stay options well signposted
•PUBLIC TOILETS•	At Church Close car park and at country park

BACKGROUND TO THE WALK

If Caspar Wistar were alive today, a springtime visit to Broadway would give him much pleasure. Visitors come in swarms to this Worcestershire village which lies against the edge of the Cotswolds – understandably, for it is one of the sweetest places in England. They buzz around a linear honeycomb, the honey-stone buildings stretching for the best part of a mile (1.6km). Horse chestnut trees flame with pinky-red candelabras and walls drip with the brilliant lilac flowers of wisteria. Caspar, the 18th-century American anatomist after whom the wisteria genus was named, would surely not miss this photo opportunity. (The fact that wisteria and pink horse chestnut are not 'authentic', as both were introduced to Britain centuries after Broadway's older buildings were constructed, doesn't seem to matter.) There are many buildings of note in Broadway, not least the partly 14th-century Lygon (pronounced 'Liggon') Arms. The Savoy Group bought it for £4.7 million in 1986. History has contributed to this price – in 1651 Oliver Cromwell stayed there on the night before the decisive clash in the Civil War, the Battle of Worcester.

Arts and Crafts

Less historic but more affordable is Broadway Tower. The 6th Earl of Coventry's four-storey folly (1799) has served as home to a printing press and a farmhouse, but is best known as a country retreat for William Morris (1834–96). Appropriately, in 1877, he founded the Society for the Protection of Ancient Buildings.

Artistically, Morris empathised with the Pre-Raphaelite Brotherhood, a group, primarily of painters, founded in 1849 by William Holman Hunt. They believed that British art had taken a 'wrong turn' under the influence of Raphael, who, with Michelangelo and Leonardo da Vinci, had made up the trio of most famous Renaissance artists. Raphael (1483–1520) was catapulted to fame and fortune in his late-twenties when commissioned to paint the stanze (Papal apartments) for Pope Julius II. The English Pre-Raphaelites challenged the teachings of the establishment, producing vividly coloured paintings, lit unconventionally, which had an almost flat appearance.

In 1859, the middle-class Morris married Jane, an 18-year-old, working-class model for Dante Gabriel Rossetti, his British-born mentor. Rossetti's wife committed suicide after two years of their marriage. Rossetti then proceeded to have an affair with Jane. Morris and some friends (including Rossetti!) set up a company producing crafted textile and stained-glass products. Morris was fascinated by pre-industrial techniques. Ironically, only the wealthy could afford to enjoy his essentially medieval art. Disillusioned by the Industrial Revolution, he was attracted to Socialism in the 1870s. He joined the Social Democratic Federation and became increasingly militant. He wrote extensively on Socialism and gave lectures, even on street corners. All the while he was writing prose and poetry and, when Tennyson died in 1892, Morris was invited to succeed him as poet laureate. He declined the invitation and died four years later.

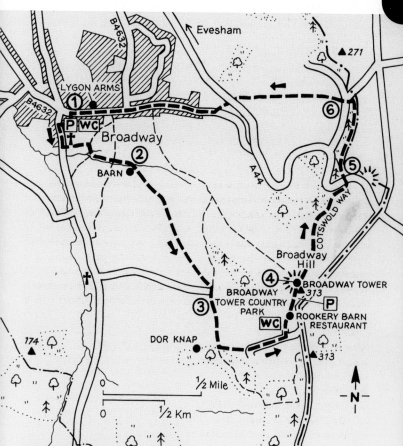

Walk 1 Directions

① Walk back down **Church Close** then turn left. At the far end of the church wall turn left, soon passing a tiny, narrow orchard. At a gate

before a strip of grass turn immediately right, to reach a simple log bridge over a rivulet. Turn half left, across uneven pasture. Go to the right-hand field corner. In 40yds (37m) reach a bridge of two railway sleepers beside a stone **barn**.

WHERE TO EAT AND DRINK ⓘ

Part-way round the route, the **Rookery Barn Restaurant** welcomes walkers (and chess players). Apart from teas and coffees, call in here for simple meals, including a vegetarian ratatouille lasagne. Dogs are welcome – above a bowl of water was chalked the sign 'Water 4 mutleys'. You can sit outside, by the adjacent children's play area. Otherwise, options abound in busy Broadway.

② Cross this to a waymarker through a boggy patch to two stiles. Maintain your line to reach a gate. Cross a large field, now scarcely gaining any height. On joining a vague, sunken lane bear right, to descend briefly to a gate (there's a water trough near by). A tree-lined, dirt track soon reaches another gate within 60yds (55m).

③ Slant uphill, passing in front of a stone building with, sadly, modern windows – **Dor Knap** (close by) is better. At the woodland ahead turn left. Join a tarmac road, steadily uphill. At the brow turn left, into **Broadway Tower Country Park**, and pass the **Rookery Barn Restaurant**. A tall kissing gate gives access to **Broadway Tower**.

④ Beyond the tower go through a similar gate, then take the little gate immediately on the right. Move down, left, 20yds (18m) to walk in a hollow, through pasture and scrubby hawthorns, to a gate in a dry-stone wall. Soon cross a tractor track and walk parallel to it in a similar hollow, guided by **Cotswold Way** acorn waymarkers. Aim for some bright metal gates among trees. Beyond these go straight ahead and in 45yds (41m), at the next marker, bear right, walking above the road. Soon cross it carefully, to footpath signs opposite.

⑤ Leave the Cotswold Way here. More care is needed in following these next instructions: descend, initially using wooden steps. Ignore a path on the left after 50yds (46m), then after another 50yds (46m) take the yellow arrow waymarker pointing up to the right, over more steps. About 25 paces beyond these steps use a wooden handrail to go down a few more steps. After another 50yds (46m) you'll see an orange **Badger Trail** disc. Go forward on this for just 10yds (9m). Here the orange disc points left, but take the yellow marker, straight ahead. Follow this narrow path (beware many exposed tree roots) near the top of this dense wood. Eventually take steps on the left, down to cross a road junction.

⑥ Take the field path signposted 'Broadway'. Descend sweetly through pastures. Swing left then right to pass under the new road, emerging near the top end of the old one. Turn right, on to the dead end of **Broadway**'s main street. In the centre, 50yds (46m) beyond three red telephone boxes, turn left, through an arcade, to **Church Close** car park.

WHILE YOU'RE THERE ⓘ

The four flights of stairs up the **Broadway Tower** add little to the already splendid view but inside it's crammed full of history (fee; closed Monday to Friday from November to March). Directly on the route is the **Wild Ridge Farm Park**, one of the country park's trinity of attractions. You don't have to be a child (or even with children) to enjoy an hour in this modest, hands-on farm park, sited on slopes overlooking the Vale of Evesham. The larger animals include wallabies, llamas, and belted Galloway cattle (a breed distinguished by a wide stripe of white around the torso of its otherwise black body).

A Fruity Route Along Cleeve Hill

A low, wooded ridge looks over a rich, fertile plain where the popular Victoria plum is grown in abundance.

•DISTANCE•	4½ miles (7.2km)
•MINIMUM TIME•	2hrs
•ASCENT / GRADIENT•	225ft (69m) ▲ ▲ ▲
•LEVEL OF DIFFICULTY•	犬犬 犬犬 犬犬
•PATHS•	Paths across fields, stony tracks and village roads, 8 stiles
•LANDSCAPE•	Level farmland with distant hills
•SUGGESTED MAP•	aqua3 OS Explorer 205 Stratford-upon-Avon & Evesham
•START / FINISH•	Grid reference: SP 077469
•DOG FRIENDLINESS•	On leads near sheep; some freedom in arable fields
•PARKING•	Outside Littleton Village Hall on School Lane, Middle Littleton, or village street (tithe barn parking for visitors only)
•PUBLIC TOILETS•	None on route

BACKGROUND TO THE WALK

The Vale of Evesham, renowned for its fruit, is virtually flat, but the growers who farm the land are constantly of the opinion that the economic 'field' on which they 'play' slopes against them. The most frequently cited objection is that producers abroad get (more) governmental assistance, facilitating a large supply of cheaper imported fruit, which consumers are willing to accept.

Plums with such evocative names as Pershore Purple and Pershore Yellow Egg used to dominate the region, but nowadays the Victoria accounts for three-quarters of the commercially grown plums. The plum is the first tree to come into flower in spring, showing its delicate white petals even before the sloe (blackthorn).

According to folklore, plums may, apparently, be used to make a love potion. In my experience, however, they are vastly more effective as a laxative than as an aphrodisiac, and I never eat prunes!

Tunnel Vision

One of the ways in which cherry growers have made themselves more competitive is to grow the fruit on dwarfing rootstocks; as the name suggests, this means that the tree does not grow to any great height, making the other labour-costly task of picking the fruit much easier. A further benefit is that the smaller trees can be covered by a plastic tunnel. Although there are now several types of plastic tunnel, in England the so-called 'French tunnel' has been around, coincidentally, since roughly the time that the Channel Tunnel began to be drilled. Such a substantial investment is best thought of as an insurance policy, protecting the fruit from summer rainstorms.

There is considerable potential to be realised from combining these two simple technologies. Perhaps other trees, such as peaches, almonds, apricots and figs, will be grown in tunnels if suitable dwarf rootstocks can be cultivated.

Walk 2

Shaping the Future

Although growers are anxious to have soft fruits such as strawberries available early in the season, it is also an advantage to be able to prolong the season. This is achieved by taking plants out of the ground during the shortest days of December and January, then arresting their growth by keeping them in cold storage (which of course incurs a cost) until required, not planting out the last until August.

On our behalf, supermarket buyers make the assumption that we will only eat perfectly proportioned strawberries. Hives of honey bees are routinely used to maximise levels of pollination (► Walk 48). Two separate studies have suggested that honey bees also reduce the percentage of misshapen fruit from about 30 per cent to below 5 per cent… presumably, as you read this, somebody is trying to work out why!

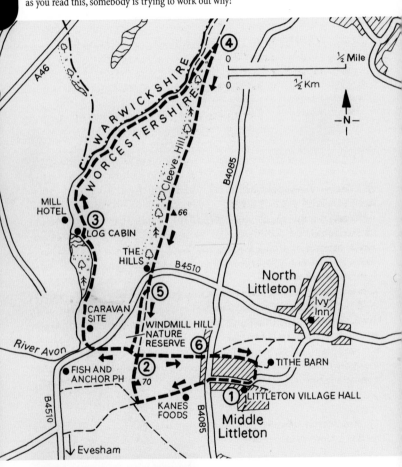

Walk 2 Directions

① Walk westwards up **School Lane** to the B4085, here called **Cleeve Road**. Cross diagonally left to take a rutted, stony track, screened by a hedgerow from **Kanes Foods**. At a junction of tracks turn right to pass beside a gate, following a blue arrow. After 328yds (300m) reach an opening on the right and a line of plum trees making a field boundary; on the left is a stile.

② Climb over this stile, entering Worcestershire Wildlife Trust's **Windmill Hill Nature Reserve**. Descend, ignoring crossing tracks, to another stile and across one field to the **B4510**. Follow the signposted 'Cleeve Prior' footpath through the caravan site. (Keep on the road for 220yds/201m for the **Fish and Anchor**.) Take a stile out of the caravan park to walk on a stone track beside the river.

WHAT TO LOOK FOR ⓘ

As you walk through the caravan site you may notice that they are raised, standing on **breeze-block pillars** about 3ft (1m) high. This is a flood protection measure. It seems that a compromise was reached with the site's insurers, for this elevation would do little to save the caravans from a repeat of the 1998 flood.

---

③ At a fenced **log cabin** with lanterns, a satellite TV dish and a basketball net, move to the right to take a double-stiled footbridge – do not be deterred by a ragged sign 'OPAC Private Fishing' – and resume your riverside stroll. Opposite, in season, you'll see the Mill Hotel's guests quaffing on the lawn. Continue through mostly ungated pastures. Through a small iron gate, leave the river by taking the right-hand fork. Ascend through trees to a clearing and a path junction.

④ Turn sharply right, back on yourself, soon walking into trees again, to follow a popular

bridleway. In a shade under 1 mile (1.6km) the **B4510** cuts through the hill, beside **The Hills**. Cross over to a fingerpost, but follow the path for just 75yds (69m).

⑤ Climb the stile into the nature reserve here, and follow the waymarked, contouring path, giving fine views westwards. After 440yds (402m) you will recognise your outward route. Turn left here, up the bank, retracing your steps for just 30yds (27m), to Point ②. Once at the top go straight across, walking with the line of plum trees on your left. When this ends maintain this direction to the **B4085**, the tithe barn making a clear objective ahead.

⑥ Cross the road and go straight ahead. Before some young trees take a stile or gate to the right. In 15yds (14m) turn left to visit the **tithe barn**, or turn right to reach the village road. Turn right again, shortly to reach your car at the start of the walk.

WHERE TO EAT AND DRINK ⓘ

Rather early on in the walk, and just a couple of minutes off the route, is the **Fish and Anchor**, which welcomes both dogs and children. South Littleton has a **post office stores** and a **fish and chip shop**, open Wednesdays to Saturdays at lunchtimes and from 5PM. In North Littleton the **Ivy Inn** serves hot food and cask ales. You may sit outside beside a green. It also has some children's play equipment and a skittle alley.

WHILE YOU'RE THERE ⓘ

In the 1970s the **Middle Littleton Tithe Barn**, once used for tithe payments to the Abbey of Evesham (► Walk 5), was lovingly restored. It's open from 2PM to 5PM (April to October), so time your walk so as not to miss it. Documents show that the barn was in use in about 1370, but carbon dating puts its construction nearly 100 years earlier. Eleven magnificent bays span its 136ft (41m) length – that's about two cricket wickets – and the apex of its roof is over 40ft (12m) above its stone-slabbed floor.

Walk 3

The Ups and Downs of Tardebigge Flight

Visit Worcestershire's famous big wet steps, steeped in economic history.

•DISTANCE•	5½ miles (8.8km)
•MINIMUM TIME•	2hrs 30min
•ASCENT / GRADIENT•	295ft (90m) ▲▲ ▲ ▲
•LEVEL OF DIFFICULTY•	🚶🚶 🚶🚶 🚶
•PATHS•	Tow path, pastures, field paths and minor lanes, 21 stiles
•LANDSCAPE•	Generally rolling rural scenery, and whole lot of locks
•SUGGESTED MAP•	aqua3 OS Explorer 204 Worcester & Droitwich Spa
•START / FINISH•	Grid reference: SO 974682
•DOG FRIENDLINESS•	Off-lead on tow path, under control in fields, lots of stiles
•PARKING•	Limited space, so park tightly and considerately, on north and east side of road bridge
•PUBLIC TOILETS•	None on route

BACKGROUND TO THE WALK

In some respects the British are a nation of slow learners: how often do we hear of a large construction project for which the final bill was vastly in excess of the original projected cost? The canal builders of the 19th century were often not much better. In 1791 an Act of Parliament gave the go-ahead to build the Worcester and Birmingham Canal, setting aside £180,000. It was only in 1815 – 24 years later – that the route to Worcester was available to commercial traffic, and the sum that had been spent was a whopping £610,000. It seems that cost projections were invariably optimistic, rather than realistic. Even at that price, the project had been scaled down, literally, for the plan to take the larger barges that plied the Severn was abandoned.

The Tardebigge Challenge

The Tardebigge Flight was just one of the challenges of constructing the Worcester and Birmingham Canal. The tally of locks along the 16-mile (25.7km) stretch between Tardebigge and Worcester is 56. Add to that five tunnels and several reservoirs, some of which the canal builders were obliged to provide for mill owners along rivers affected by the canal, and it is not only the locks that escalate!

Stoke Prior Salt Works

The Worcester and Birmingham Canal benefited from the discovery of salt at Stoke Prior in 1825 – the salt works were built around the canal shortly after. The works are still clearly visible on the suggested map; note in particular the 'Reservoir (brine)' at grid ref SO 947664. This was the works that John Corbett (► Walk 11) purchased in 1845.

While he must take the credit for the subsequent pre-eminence of his factory there, he must have been assisted by the competition between canal and railway. The Birmingham and Gloucester Railway had opened in 1841, and in 1851 another line followed: the Oxford, Worcester and Wolverhampton Railway.

Back in 1771, long before the Worcester and Birmingham Canal was conceived, James Brindley had engineered the broad-beamed Droitwich Barge Canal, right into the town's salt production centre. It ran for 5¾ miles (9.2km) to the River Severn, taking salt down and bringing coal up. Perhaps as a response to the railway threat, this 'cul-de-sac' was opened up in 1853 by cutting a mere 1½ mile (2.4km) narrow-beamed channel from the centre of Droitwich to Hanbury Wharf, joining the Droitwich Barge Canal with the Worcester and Birmingham Canal – the so-called Droitwich Junction Canal. Transportation of salt by canal ceased in 1914.

Even if you are not a canal-boat lover, the Tardebigge Flight is a memorable spectacle – it just goes on and on. It has a total of 30 locks within 2 miles (3.2km). There are 17 at the start of the route (if you choose Walk 4) and 13 at the end.

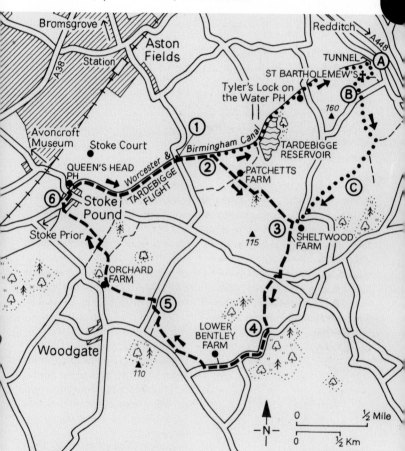

Walk 3 Directions

① Cross **bridge No 51** and turn left, taking the tow path on the south side. Follow this to a point about 15yds (14m) before the next

bridge – No 52. (The Walk 4 extension begins here.)

② Turn right here, into some trees, then down a field. Cross a double-stiled footbridge among trees then keep straight ahead, over the

Walk 3

driveway to **Patchetts Farm**. Skirt a copse to the left, then another stile and a two-plank bridge. Cross two more fields, keeping a hedge on your left. You will come to a gate on your left, close to a broken oak tree with a substantial girth. (Walk 4 rejoins here.)

③ Turn right. Within 110yds (100m) go through the gate ahead (no waymarker), ignoring one to the left. Go a quarter right (or skirt the crops) to find a stile. Retain this diagonal to cross a simple footbridge of three planks, then find a rickety, narrow stile in the next field's corner. Walk with the hedge on your left to reach a minor road junction. Turn right for about 55yds (50m). Turn left to walk across three more fields to a

dilapidated metal gate. Now take the right-hand field edge to reach a minor road.

④ Turn right. Follow this for ½ mile (800m) to **Lower Bentley Farm**'s driveway. Go 140yds (128m) further, to a fingerpost on the right. Cross pastures by gaps in hedgerows, later with a hedge on your left, but veer to a stile in the right-hand corner at the end. Cross this, then a double stile, go three-quarters left to a road.

⑤ Turn right, and in 75yds (69m) turn left. Here, beyond a very awkward ditch, is a new kissing gate with a latch. Cross pastures easily towards **Orchard Farm**, but then turn right, away from it. Over the corner stile go straight ahead. At a double stile (across a ditch) go half left, and at a gap in the hedge turn right. Now turn left without gaining height for 650yds (594m), aiming to the left of a black-and-white house, for a stile and gate. In 80yds (73m) reach a road.

⑥ Turn right. At the T-junction turn left. Join the canal tow path this side of the **Stoke Pound Bridge**. (The **Queen's Head** is on the other side.) Now you have over ¾ mile (1.2km) to return to your car at the road bridge, approximately mid-way up the **Tardebigge Flight**.

Tardebigge – Seeing the Complete Picture

To view all of the locks of the Tardebigge Flight, see the reservoir and look through the tunnel, take this extension.
See map and information panel for Walk 3

•DISTANCE•	7¾ miles (12.5km)
•MINIMUM TIME•	3hrs 15min
•ASCENT / GRADIENT•	380ft (115m) ▲▲▲
•LEVEL OF DIFFICULTY•	秋 秋 秋

Walk 4 Directions (Walk 3 option)

Keep on the tow path at Point ② and continue to follow it for a little over 1¼ miles (2km). At a bend the embankment of the **Tardebigge Reservoir** looms. Whenever a boat passes through a lock, heading either up or down, a lockful of water is shunted downstream by gravity. Although the locks are not built any wider or longer than is necessary, maintaining an adequate flow of water can be a problem at any time, not just when there is a dry summer. Hence the need for the reservoir, approached from its dammed end.

Beyond the topmost lock of the 30 is another striking feat of engineering – **Tardebigge Tunnel**, Point Ⓐ. Turn right through a kissing gate just before the tunnel, but first descend steps to the tow path to see the light at the tunnel's far portal, 580yds (530m) away. Doubtless some of the extra money went into the making of this tunnel, which was bored through solid rock.

Bear right, up the bank, with the distinctive, Baroque needle spire of **St Bartholomew's** ahead. The tower was completed in 1777. Cross the gravel car park then walk past the church it serves. Walk with the **primary school** on your left for just 30yds (27m). Turn left, beside the school and later its playing field, to reach a minor road, Point Ⓑ.

Cross the road by a kissing gate and then a stile. Maintain a line across four fields, keeping the field boundary on your left. In the small, fifth field bear right a little, to reach a stile with yellow waymarkers giving two options in the big field ahead. The line you require is the right-hand fork, but it is simpler to walk to the gate straight ahead of you then, instead of going through it, walk with the hedge on your left, eventually reaching a stile in the far corner, Point Ⓒ. Cross a double stile into the next field. At the end of a copse cross a stile on the right to reach a minor road. Turn left here in the direction of **Sheltwood Farm**, but in 25yds (23m) go through a gate on the right-hand side. Walk across this field, then go through another gate to rejoin Walk 3 at Point ③.

Walk 5

Badsey's Wartime Memories

A circuit from Badsey, where German prisoners of war helped feed the nation.

·DISTANCE·	4½ miles (7.2km)
·MINIMUM TIME·	2hrs
·ASCENT / GRADIENT·	80ft (24m)
·LEVEL OF DIFFICULTY·	
·PATHS·	Meadow and arable paths, tracks and minor lanes, 26 stiles
·LANDSCAPE·	Flat, market gardening and pasture
·SUGGESTED MAP·	aqua3 OS Explorer 205 Stratford-upon-Avon & Evesham
·START / FINISH·	Grid reference: SP 070431
·DOG FRIENDLINESS·	Can be off lead away from sheep pastures
·PARKING·	Roadside parking, Badsey village
·PUBLIC TOILETS·	None on route

Walk 5 Directions

Walk south from **St James' Church**, close to the village stores and post office. Turn left, past the **Wheatsheaf** and along **School Lane** then right into **Willersey Road**. After 150yds (137m), turn left into **Sands Lane**. Walk for 500yds (457m), passing **Greenacres Animal Rescue**, to take a fingerpost, right, opposite the freedom paddocks. Follow waymarkers to a lane.

This is market gardening country. During the First World War at least 20 locations in Worcestershire were used to house prisoners of war (POWs), as part of the Government's drive to plug the gap left in the farming economy by those who had been sent away to

fight. Badsey's POWs were mostly employed by market gardeners – the most labour-intensive of agricultural activities – at a time of low mechanisation.

At the lane turn right for nearly ½ mile (800m). When this bends right, go straight ahead on a track. After ¼ mile (400m), just after some low corrugated iron sheds, take a stile on the right-hand side (or go ahead, then left at the main road, to visit the **Sandys Arms**). More meadow stiles lead to Wickhamford's memorial hall.

Turn right, passing striking black-and-white houses, some thatched. After 275yds (251m), at a right-hand bend, go left, passing the spectacular **Wickhamford Manor House**, to pass in front of St John the Baptist Church, of weathered sandstone with a squat tower. A footbridge crosses **Badsey Brook**; follow the left-hand field edge.

All the market garden produce had to be collected. Basket-making was a specific skill held by some of the

> **WHERE TO EAT AND DRINK** ⓘ
> In Badsey the **Wheatsheaf** serves food (but not on Sunday evening). The **village stores** is open seven days a week and has supplies to get you round the walk. In Wickhamford the **Sandys Arms** is a worthy detour on a hot day.

POWs, and was particularly welcomed by their new employers. The POWs themselves received 1*d* of the 4*d* their employers had to pay to the Government for their services. In fact, 4*d* became 5*d* after grumblings were made about these employers having access to preferential rates.

Beside a black wooden shed, join a green-centred track to **Badsey Lane**. Cross to take a similar track to **Badsey Road**. Cross this, taking the road through Aldington to a junction, past the imposing house and in front of **The Old Stables**. Turn right then almost immediately left, now on **Chapel Lane**. Just after the last house go half right, to a footbridge. Over this, cross one field then, in a plantation, is the walk's only ascent, far less taxing than the vicious tree stumps on the path itself. From this elevation Badsey is just to the south, and more distantly is Broadway Tower on Broadway Hill.

The Manor House in Badsey was built to house monks from Evesham Abbey who fell sick. A striking black-and-white private residence, parts of it date to about 1350, but it is mostly 16th-century. Now flanked by modern, functional houses, it is, architecturally, an oasis. Towards the end of the First World War the Manor House, then a boys' home, was requisitioned to accommodate POWs.

It's debatable how closely a local (and parochial) newspaper reflects the views of its mainstream readership, and so much has changed since that time. Pockets of resentment certainly existed, for example, the 'local rag' gave a dressing-down to a farmer who

gave cider to his workers, among whom were German POWs. Hatred there may have been, but perhaps it was more for the war itself than the individuals who had been flung into it unwittingly.

Although some prisoners attempted to escape, such stories are rare. What was the incentive? Despite the mental strain of being a prisoner abroad, and living in what must have been cramped conditions – according to an edition of the *Evesham Journal*, about 100 men were held in the Manor House – to be captured, uninjured, and taken away from the front to do essentially familiar, physical work was a dream ticket when set alongside the hell of trench life.

> **WHAT TO LOOK FOR** ⓘ
>
> Between Wickhamford and Aldington you'll see a long row of water outlets for the intensive **market gardening** here. Immediately after this, a black wooden shed shows the April 1998 flood level, about 3ft (1m) above the field level. Look out for all manner of produce in season – rhubarb, lettuce, spinach, broccoli, beetroot, courgettes, pumpkins and leeks.

In front of a dark green barn turn right. At the **B4085** go right for just 40yds (37m). Turn right and down this meadow to find a footbridge. Veer left a little to a rickety stile beside a shed with barbed-wire gates policed by alsatians. A green-middled track leads to **Badsey Road**. Turn right then left to view the **Manor House** on the right.

Continue along this street to the start at **St James' Church**, where the Manor House's POWs frequently attended services and had their own choir.

Chilled Orange Juice at Hanbury Hall

A stroll around an estate park, with an opportunity to visit a rejuvenated country house, its outbuildings and its gardens.

•DISTANCE•	4¾ miles (7.7km)
•MINIMUM TIME•	2hrs 15min
•ASCENT / GRADIENT•	250ft (76m) ▲▲ ▲ ▲
•LEVEL OF DIFFICULTY•	🚶 🚶 🚶
•PATHS•	Meadows, tracks and easy woodland paths, 17 stiles
•LANDSCAPE•	Parkland, woodland, country house
•SUGGESTED MAP•	aqua3 OS Explorer 204 Worcester & Droitwich Spa
•START / FINISH•	Grid reference: SO 957652
•DOG FRIENDLINESS•	Not good; not allowed in Hanbury Hall's garden (or house), lots of sheep
•PARKING•	Piper's Hill car park, on B4091 between Stoke Works and Hanbury (fast road and no sign)
•PUBLIC TOILETS•	None on route

BACKGROUND TO THE WALK

To my mind, the contraceptive pill, the motor car and the television were the three most socially influential inventions of modern times. Further down the list, but a candidate for a top ten position, would come the domestic refrigerator. The commercial exploitation of the refrigeration principle was not realised until 1877, when the world's first refrigerated ship, equipped with a system designed by Frenchman Ferdinand Carré, brought frozen meat to France from Argentina. The now ubiquitous fridge-freezer did not begin mass production until much later, at a General Electric factory in 1939.

Ice Houses

Prior to this refrigeration, the only way of keeping things cold was to use ice. It was stored in ice wells or ice houses. When ice was not available, salting, ► Walk 11, was the primary method of preserving meat. Records show that Britain imported ice by ship from Scandinavia right up until 1921, a trade that had begun about 100 years earlier. Before that time it was collected in the winter from any practicable place – ponds, rivers and canals, and even by crushing snow. The ice house at Hanbury Hall is a wonderful specimen. It's a shame that there aren't enough volunteers around to bring it back into use once more.

Built in the mid-18th century, it was sunk 11ft (3.5m) into the ground and topped with a mound of earth. Internally it is 20ft (6m) high and over 15ft (4.6m) across, making it roughly egg-shaped – clever brickwork of which Stephen Ballard (► Walk 27) would have been proud. The dome has a hatch in it (now covered with perspex, providing a useful skylight) and the entrance is a corridor nearly 28ft (8.5m) long. Melted ice drains through a grid in the brick floor.

To some extent it was possible to manufacture ice. Close to the ice house, two deep pools with sluice gates served as reservoirs and, on frosty nights, water would be released into a third, shallow pool, yielding an ice 'crop' to be cut the next morning. Additionally, after heavy snowfalls, all available hands were put to shovels. The snow was compressed using feet, and then flung down the hatch.

Orangery

The Orangery at Hanbury Hall is a wide, nine-bay building, with a lot of glass at the front – sufficient to protect oranges and other frost-sensitive plants from all but the harshest of winters. Architecturally, its highlights are the intricate carvings of fruit and foliage. Built in the 1740s, it was on its own until the 1770s extension to the gardens embraced it. Over the past ten years the gardens at Hanbury Hall have been, not restored, but largely recreated in their original design, using detailed documentation and, when necessary, best guesses.

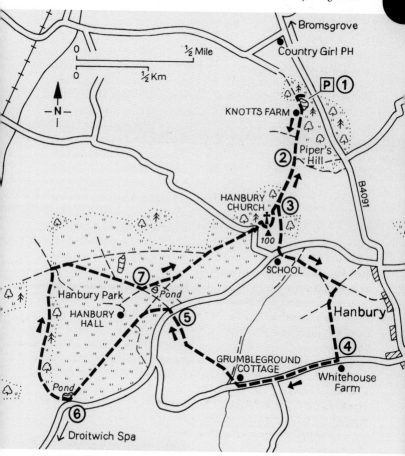

Walk 6 Directions

① From the bottom of the car park, follow the driveway to **Knotts Farm**. Go ahead on the left-hand one of two seemingly parallel paths.

About 350yds (320m) after the farm reach a gravel track at a fingerpost.

② Go straight ahead, with a field boundary on your left. Ascending towards the church, reach a stake with two waymarkers.

Walk 6

③ Fork left, soon passing a spinney, then losing height across a meadow. Take care as the stile and steps here spill you straight on to a minor but fast road. Across this, go beside the school. Ahead, when 20yds (18m) before a stile out of the third field, turn right, aiming just to the left of a young, fenced oak. Cross a wobbly stile. In 70yds (64m) cross a footbridge on the left. Two more stiles lead to **Pumphouse Lane**.

④ Turn right. Take a stile and gate close to the black-and-white **Grumbleground Cottage**. In 40yds (37m) cross a three-plank footbridge. Ascend slightly, in line with electricity poles. After two fields turn right, alongside a wire fence. Reach a road.

⑤ Cross the road to the footpath opposite. At a stile go half left, guided by a solitary, fenced conifer. Pass close to **Hanbury Hall**'s entrance, easing away from the perimeter wall to cross a large field to a corner. (Autumn leaves hanging over the pond here are a picture.)

⑥ Ignore the minor road, turning immediately right. Hug the boundary fence of the coppice. Continue down the right-hand field edge. At a junction turn right at a National Trust sign, into this former deer park. After just 50yds (46m), at a small drainage ditch, edge right, along a slight green hollow. After another 110yds (100m), where it curves right, leave this hollow to keep your line. Aim for a stile about 300yds (274m) away, to the left of a clump of fenced trees, which hides a round pond. Maintain this line going up the incline – Hanbury church is seen on the left – to reach a tarmac driveway.

⑦ Turn left. When it curves right go straight ahead to walk in an oak avenue. Keep this line for 700yds (640m), to a minor road. Turn right, then left up to the **church**. In the churchyard walk round the perimeter, down to a kissing gate. Shortly rejoin the outward route at Point ③. Remember to go left, into the woods, at Point ②.

Breathing Space in the Clent Hills

A brief circuit of the most visited hills in Worcestershire where, in springtime, fields of oilseed rape flood the landscape with colour.

•DISTANCE•	3½ miles (5.7km)
•MINIMUM TIME•	2hrs
•ASCENT / GRADIENT•	660ft (200m) ▲ ▲ ▲
•LEVEL OF DIFFICULTY•	👫 👫 👫
•PATHS•	Woodland paths (sometimes muddy), tracks, 8 stiles
•LANDSCAPE•	Mixture of urban cityscape and rolling rural scenery
•SUGGESTED MAP•	aqua3 OS Explorer 219 Wolverhampton & Dudley
•START / FINISH•	Grid reference: SO 938808
•DOG FRIENDLINESS•	Plenty of running on tops, under control near livestock
•PARKING•	National Trust pay-and-display car park, Nimmings Wood
•PUBLIC TOILETS•	At start

BACKGROUND TO THE WALK

If you are a visitor to Worcestershire then the Clent Hills provide an excellent starting point. More people visit the Clent Hills than Worcester Cathedral. Three car parks provide easy access and make the hills the county's number one non-paying attraction. Of course, proximity to the West Midlands conurbation has much to do with it, but there is something satisfying in standing on the top as dusk falls, watching the city lights begin to sparkle in the distance.

Yellow Spring

Come up to the ridge along the Clent Hills in late April or early May and you may see not only vertical grey blocks of suburban Birmingham, but horizontal yellow blocks of modern rural Worcestershire, created by the flowers of oilseed rape. In 1971 the amount of oilseed rape grown in Britain was a mere 12,500 acres (5,062ha), but it increased 20-fold in the following decade and by 2001 was a staggering 3.2 million acres (1.3 million ha). Daffodils aside, it is now the main source of early spring colour in the countryside – Worcestershire and Herefordshire are no exceptions.

Fashionably Sensible

The plant, a brassica, derives its unfortunate name from the Latin word for turnip, *rapum* (whereas the verb comes from *rapere*, to snatch). Rapeseed oil is just one of many vegetable oils grown for human consumption. If your food has to be fried then it is both fashionable and good advice to cook using rapeseed oil – not only is it without cholesterol (as are all vegetable oils), but of the known vegetable oils it is the one with the lowest level of saturated fatty acids.

In spite of all this nutritional worthiness, however, only about 40 per cent of the rapeseed oil goes into cooking-oil production, for it is used in a number of industrial applications too, such as lubricants.

White Honey

Oilseed rape typically begins to flower in mid-April – earlier than traditional crops – for a 5–6 week period, so beekeepers have to mobilise their bees earlier, to exploit the available nectar (► Walk 48). The nectar sets very quickly, so the beekeeper must extract it from the honeycomb just as the yellow hue is turning to green. Honey derived primarily from oilseed rape is almost white, has a soft texture, and a comparatively bland favour. So much oilseed rape is now grown that it has taken over from white clover as the country's largest source of honey, although some say that white clover produced the best honey (which is not white but pale straw in colour), especially when it grew in long-established, permanent pasture.

Walk 7 **Directions**

① Return to the car park entrance and turn right for a few paces. Cross the road to a stile and take the left-hand of two options. Immediately you'll see a striking urban panorama. Descend steadily

but, at a cylindrical wooden post, turn right (with a waymarker). Continue across fields, probably populated with horses, until a kissing gate. Here take the forward option (not the right fork), to reach the churchyard of **St Kenelm's** in Romsley parish. It may appear 'overgrown' since, like the churchyard of St Michael at Dulas (► Walk 41), it is managed like a traditional hay meadow.

② Leave by the lychgate. Turn left along the road for a short distance, then right when you reach the T-junction. In about 125yds (114m) take the waymarked path at the driveway to **The Wesleys** to ascend gently. Turn left on to a tarmac road. Ignore the left turn but, just 30yds (27m) beyond it, take a muddy, narrow path into woodland up on the right, angled away from the road and not signposted. Emerge from the trees to the trig point on **Walton Hill**. Turn left, taking the right-hand of the two options. Follow this for ¾ mile (1.2km) until just 10yds (9m) beyond a National Trust marker post. Here take the right-hand fork to a stile. Go steeply down two meadows to the road beside the **Church of St Leonard's** in Clent.

③ Turn right then right again. At **Church View Cottage**, opposite the church's driveway, turn left. In 125yds (114m) take the upper, left fork. In 90yds (82m), at a crossing, go left. After a further 100yds (91m) ignore options to turn right or half right. Proceed for a further 120yds (110m). Do not climb the stile on your left but go straight on, soon ascending steeply up wooden steps. After another 100yds (91m) you'll emerge from the trees. Now cross a track then turn right.

④ Keep on this broad, open path, passing close to (or viewing) a toposcope beside four standing stones. Maintain this line to descend in woodland to the road. Just on the left is the car park at the start of the walk.

Walk 8

Bracing Bredon Hill

A walk on Bredon Hill and through Worcestershire's perry country.

•DISTANCE•	7½ miles (12.1km)
•MINIMUM TIME•	3hrs 30min
•ASCENT / GRADIENT•	1,115ft (340m) ▲▲▲
•LEVEL OF DIFFICULTY•	𝕉𝕉 𝕉𝕉 𝕉
•PATHS•	Tracks, woodland paths, bridleways, minor lanes, 11 stiles
•LANDSCAPE•	Farmland, woodland, panoramic views into Wales
•SUGGESTED MAP•	aqua3 OS Explorer 190 Malvern Hills & Bredon Hill
•START / FINISH•	Grid reference: SO 955423
•DOG FRIENDLINESS•	Close control needed – cows, horses and lots of sheep
•PARKING•	Roadside parking, Great Comberton village
•PUBLIC TOILETS•	None on route

BACKGROUND TO THE WALK

Bredon Hill is a solitary outcrop of hard, yellowish limestone. The fort on its plateau summit enclosed 22 acres (8.9ha). Today the hill is one of English Nature's National Nature Reserves.

Pershore's Pears

As the name Pershore – 'Pearshore' – suggests, the area around nearby Pershore has long been synonymous with pears (and plums too – ▶ Walk 2). Although perry remains a popular drink, with some manufacturers of perry apparently planting new orchards, many traditional pear orchards have, like apple orchards, been wiped off the map, either for more lucrative forms of agricultural activity, or for house building. An interesting legacy is the presence of pear trees in local hedgerows.

The pear's gene pool is being maintained by setting up a national collection. As many as 120 varieties of perry pear have been recorded; about half of these have been traced in recent years. Specimens have been planted at the Three Counties Showground, near Malvern. In addition, the Worcestershire County Council's Conservation and Landscape Team runs a fruit-tree scheme, like its counterpart in Herefordshire (▶ Walk 31). Pear, along with other fruit trees such as cherry, apple and plum, is a popular wood for turnery; also, the fine grain of pear wood makes it an acceptable substitute for engraving when the favoured box wood is not available.

When you are in Worcester (▶ Walk 12) look out for the city's coat of arms – it bears three black pears. The story goes that when Queen Elizabeth I visited Worcester, the city's 16th-century events manager arranged for a Worcester Black Pear tree to be placed along her route; this pleased Her Majesty, who pronounced that the city's coat of arms ought to display these splendid fruits … and so it came to pass. Doubtless she didn't actually taste one for, unless it has changed down the years, the fruit is a great disappointment – too tough to eat uncooked, it needs to be served in a pudding such as a crumble, or preserved in syrup. (The same goes for the colour – the fruits are no more black than white grapes are white.) Nevertheless to encourage some sense of heritage among its children, Worcestershire City Council has provided every one of the city's schools with a Worcester Black Pear tree.

Fortified

Elmley Castle's name dates from the 11th century, when Robert le Despenser built a castle on an outlier of Bredon Hill. It was later part of the estate of the Beauchamp family. The castle was again fortified in the 14th century, after interim decay. It is said that stones from this castle were used to build the old Pershore Bridge, adjacent to the present-day A44 road bridge. Today there is precious little to see of the castle itself (on private land). Although nothing like the scale of the fort, the castle's earthworks warrant portrayal on the Ordnance Survey map, and a 'castle pool' is also shown.

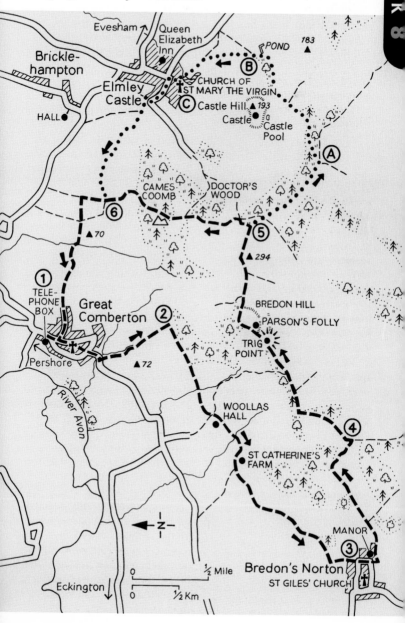

Walk 8

Walk 8 Directions

① Begin beside the telephone box in Great Comberton. Follow **Church Street**. Go through the churchyard; leave by a gate. At the road go down the stem of the T-junction. In the dip find a stile. Ascend two fields, with a stream on your left. After 100yds (91m) in the third there is a signpost.

WHILE YOU'RE THERE ⓘ

A few miles to the north and clearly seen from Bredon Hill is **Pershore Abbey** in Pershore. Founded in the 7th century, the oldest surviving parts, hewn from local limestone, are Norman.

---

② Turn right, initially beside trees. Soon a good farm track strikes across meadow. Ahead is a perfect Malverns' view. Follow waymarkers for the next 1½ miles (2.4km), taking the gravel driveway beside **Woollas Hall** and skirting **St Catherine's Farm**. Take a hard track, later tarmac, down into **Bredon's Norton**. After the first few houses reach a junction.

③ Keep ahead for 100yds (91m) to another junction. Turn right if visiting **St Giles' Church**; otherwise go ahead again, then round a left bend. Go into a field, to the right of two buildings – there's a waymarker on telegraph pole. Now follow an excellent track steadily upwards, through several gates, eventually swinging south east, for at least

---

WHAT TO LOOK FOR ⓘ

The lovely stone **Woollas Hall** is nearly 400 years old. You should see deer here, kept in by a tall fence. The (green) carpet of **St Giles' Church** in Bredon's Norton is singularly un-Norman; part of the church was rebuilt in the early 1880s.

¼ mile (1.2km). Less than 100yds (91m) beyond a single marker post reach a T-junction with 'no right of way' ahead.

④ Turn left. Soon go half right along a field edge, then right to walk along the wooded escarpment ridge, before open field leads to the triangulation pillar. Continue through the great fortifications and past an 18th-century tower called **Parson's Folly**, Mr Parson having lived at nearby Kemerton. There's a topograph here too. I could see Sugar Loaf, near Abergavenny, 49 miles (79km) away. Follow the escarpment eastwards. Pass a small plantation, then follow a wire fence, slightly descending, for over ¼ mile (400m), to a wood.

WHERE TO EAT AND DRINK ⓘ

Walk 8 is 'dry'. On Walk 9 is the **Queen Elizabeth Inn** in Elmley Castle, which welcomes children and dogs; or try the **Bell Inn**, Eckington, on the B4080.

---

⑤ Don't enter the wood; turn left, beside it. Within 150yds (137m), bend right to a junction. Turn left, down a green hollow. At **Doctor's Wood** veer left to cross an oddly level field (note the absence of contours on the suggested map). Descend steeply through **Cames Coomb**, along a wide, well-horsed path. Briefly follow a level forestry road, then leave the trees, descending on a scalpings track for 400yds (366m) to a path junction.

⑥ Walk a further 375yds (343m) on the good track to find a path on the left, initially between two hedges. When it ends go straight ahead. Keep this general line – later a hard track – back into **Great Comberton**. Turn right to the telephone box.

On to Lovely Elmley Castle

Extend your walk to visit the pretty village of Elmley Castle.
See map and information panel for Walk 8

•DISTANCE•	9¼ miles (14.9km)
•MINIMUM TIME•	4hrs 30min
•ASCENT / GRADIENT•	1,180ft (360m) ▲▲▲
•LEVEL OF DIFFICULTY•	🚶 🚶 🚶

Walk 9 Directions (Walk 8 option)

Go through the gate at Point ⑤. Walk an easy ⅝ mile (1km) on a firm, fenced path, flanked by a steep wooded slope and open fields. Where the fence kinks there are gates on the right, and Wychavon Way indicators. This is Point Ⓐ.

Go half left, into the woods, descending steadily on a wide bridle path. Leave this woodland for open meadow. Lower down, veer right, following single post waymarkers. Cross a wooden footbridge over a ditch. Continue descending through light woodland with bracken. At a possible fork go left (a wooden post waymarker soon reassures) to another footbridge. Here go left, away from the fence, passing a long and narrow pond on the right.

Within 100yds (91m) of this pond, reach a gate with blue and yellow arrows, Point Ⓑ. Follow the yellow one across a two-plank footbridge. Go three-quarters right in parkland. In the next, large field veer left (or skirt the field edge left if it's under crops) to find a stile into a small paddock, and then another stile. A wooded path crosses a decorative dammed pond. You are soon in the churchyard of St Mary the Virgin in **Elmley Castle**, Point Ⓒ.

The chancel of the church was probably built before AD 1100, a supposition based in part on the 'herringbone' style of stonework in the chancel wall. Its font has a 15th-century octagonal bowl on a 13th-century square base decorated with carved serpents and dragons. Of particular note in the church is a set of three 17th-century effigies of the Savage family, lying down, with four children kneeling before them.

Through the main church gate, go forward just 40yds (37m), then turn left (but you may first wish to explore the village). Pass several black-and-white houses, some of which are thatched. At a sharp left bend go over a stile to the right, beside a farm building. Turn left to cross a concreted area; leave the farm through two gates. Follow the right-hand field edge. In the third field, after 50yds (46m), turn three-quarters right at a redundant stile, soon regaining your line. To the right is **Bricklehampton Hall**. Continue for three fields, crossing stiles and plank bridges over ditches. Reach a scalpings track coming down from the left – here you rejoin Walk 8 at Point ⑥.

Huddington Court Terrorists

An easy ramble to see the charming den of 16th-century conspirators.

•DISTANCE•	5¼ miles (8.4km)
•MINIMUM TIME•	2hrs 30min
•ASCENT / GRADIENT•	70ft (21m) ▲▲▲
•LEVEL OF DIFFICULTY•	🚶🚶 🚶
•PATHS•	Meadows and field paths, tracks and lanes, 14 stiles
•LANDSCAPE•	Gentle farmland, picturesque, historic house
•SUGGESTED MAP•	aqua3 OS Explorer 204 Worcester & Droitwich Spa
•START / FINISH•	Grid reference: SO 943543
•DOG FRIENDLINESS•	Mixed farmland throughout
•PARKING•	Grassy area beyond school or on streets, Upton Snodsbury
•PUBLIC TOILETS•	None on route

Walk 10 Directions

Begin on the primary school road, south of **St Kenelm's Church** (1874). Go west, past the school then some bungalows. Go diagonally right, down to the **A422**, beside the **French House Inn**. Cross over. Turn left, then right after 50yds (46m). In 100yds (91m) go ahead. Walk a long field, scarcely gaining any height. Eventually leave by a narrow metal gate, not a wide wooden one higher up.

Guy Fawkes was caught red-handed in the cellars of Parliament just after midnight on the night of 4–5 November in 1605. Historians cannot agree precisely why he was doing it. Was it a (misguided) attempt to spark the reinstatement of Catholicism, or a means of tarnishing the Jesuit movement by blaming them, thus strengthening the Protestant position? Guy Fawkes was born a Protestant, but converted to Catholicism in his early 20s. Aged 23, he went to the Netherlands to become a mercenary in the Spanish army-in-residence. He apparently believed that, given the right catalyst for change, Catholics in England would overthrow the King.

Now go straight ahead, joining a driveway. When 90yds (82m) beyond Bow Brook's bridge go half-right, crossing the drive to **Manor House** by stiles in wire fences. Later, at the stile close to Manor House, go well left, crossing three fields diagonally, to a minor road. Turn right for just 55yds (50m). Now follow a right-hand field edge (fingerpost). Just before the corner go through a gap to put it on your other side. At the next corner go through a gate and turn right. At an opening into a big field aim 10yds (9m) left of a two-poled power pylon ahead. In and out of

---

WHILE YOU'RE THERE ⓘ

Adjacent to the lawn of Huddington Court is the largely Norman and 14th-century **Church of St James**. Between his arrest and execution, Robert Wintour admitted that he had told the chaplain, a Jesuit priest, about the Gunpowder Plot.

woodland, take the right-hand field edge. At the bend ignore a double stile and three-planked bridge, going 20yds (18m) further to another stile. Go diagonally, to a waymarked stile 40yds (37m) before a metal gate. Emerge beside a black-and-white house and a greenhouse, beside **Huddington Court**.

Thomas Wintour (or Winter) and his brother Robert both lived at Huddington Court. They were two of at least 13 men involved in the conspiracy. Guy Fawkes was not the principal conspirator – just inept enough to get himself caught. It is claimed that he was found by people making a search, having received a 'tip off' in the form of an anonymous letter to a prominent Catholic, Lord Monteagle.

Turn left, crossing a dam, to a minor road. In 120yds (110m) turn into the Court's driveway. When it swings right, stop to admire the house. Huddington Court was built in the early 1500s, but greatly altered in 1584. Timber-framed, it has brick chimneyshafts. The surrounding moat, which adds to its attractiveness, was probably dug for an earlier property on the site. The house belonged to the Wintours until 1658. Significantly, inside is a most secure priest-hole. Huddington Court is now privately owned. I wonder what they do on 5 November?

In his reign Henry VIII's Draconian dissolution of the monasteries had stripped them of their vast wealth, and he had established the Church of England, having broken away from the Pope. Later, Queen Elizabeth I introduced outrageous (but lucrative) fines for persons not attending Anglican services,

so-called 'recusants'. A form of 'closet Catholicism' continued – almost literally, since harbouring a Catholic priest was punishable by death, and so some of them hid in priest-holes. Europe had also been incensed by Queen Elizabeth's execution of the fleeing Scottish Queen, Mary, a Catholic, in 1587. At the time of the Gunpowder Plot, James I, the Scottish King, had just inherited the English throne after the death of Elizabeth in 1603. Those who had not been killed shortly after the discovery of Guy Fawkes were executed for treason in early 1606. These included Robert Wintour on 30 January and Thomas Wintour and Guy Fawkes on 31 January. In fact, they were hung, drawn and quartered (having probably been tortured first), then sundry body parts were exhibited.

WHERE TO EAT AND DRINK

There's a **stores and post office** in Huddington. Near the start is the **French House Inn**; with a beer garden. West a little, at the Peopleton turn, is the (residential) **Coventry Arms**.

Back at the minor road, walk on to **Mill Farm**. Follow the fingerpost. In a big field aim for a prominent ash at a far woodland corner. Walk with the plantation on your left. At its second corner, turn left. At the end of this field keep within it, turning right. In 120yds (110m) go for 500yds (457m) diagonally towards trees, passing 50yds (46m) left of the first pylon. Through an aperture in the trees, reach a stile within 50yds (46m). Go forward, then veer left, briefly hugging the fence of **Bow Wood** on your right. Towards the brow ease left, near this edge for 400yds (366m) to a gate. A stone track leads to the **A422** and thus **Upton Snodsbury** village.

Droitwich Spa: Turning Salt into Silver

A walk through an historical town where salt once made a fortune for a local family.

•DISTANCE•	5¾ miles (9.2km)
•MINIMUM TIME•	2hrs 30min
•ASCENT / GRADIENT•	230ft (70m)
•LEVEL OF DIFFICULTY•	
•PATHS•	Pavements, field paths, stony tracks, 6 stiles
•LANDSCAPE•	Agricultural lowlands, coppices, historical town
•SUGGESTED MAP•	aqua3 OS Explorer 204 Worcester & Droitwich Spa
•START / FINISH•	Grid reference: SO 898631
•DOG FRIENDLINESS•	Some country stretches but too urban to be much fun
•PARKING•	Long-stay pay-and-display between Heritage Way and Saltway (follow brown signs for 'Brine Baths')
•PUBLIC TOILETS•	St Andrews Shopping Centre

BACKGROUND TO THE WALK

Given that sea water is salty, it is not surprising to find salt pans by the Atlantic or on the Mediterranean coast. But how has salt been produced in Droitwich since prehistoric times? The answer is simply that the ground is rich in rock salt. The brine from the town's salt springs is far denser than sea water – 2½ lbs could be extracted by boiling a gallon of Droitwich's brine (about 250g from each litre).

Salinae

Droitwich was an important Roman crossroads – the suggested map shows that the A38(T), the B4090 and the minor road to the north, Crutch Lane, all have Roman origins. They had a fort at Dodderhill (just north of Vines Park), and when the railway was constructed in 1847 two mosaic pavements were stumbled upon. Later archaeological work found a Roman corridor house about 130ft (40m) long.

Salt tax was a good earner for the monarch, up until its abolition in 1825. Ownership of 25 salt-evaporating pans contributed to the wealth of the Wintour family, who gained notoriety in 1605 (► Walk 10).

The Salt King

In 1845, when aged 28, John Corbett used capital from his father's canal business's profits to buy and update a derelict salt works about 4½ miles (7.2km) north east, at Stoke Prior (► Walks 3 and 4). He did the right thing at the right time. His works, Europe's largest, made him a fortune, much of which he pumped back into the company, improving working conditions and raising wages (to the extent that wives no longer needed to work), and also into the area, Droitwich Spa in particular. In France, in 1855, he met Anna (or Hannah) O'Meara, who lived in Paris with her French mother and Irish father. Corbett married her the following year. They had six children. Such was her apparent craving for France that he commissioned an architect to build him a French château, Château Impney, completed in 1875 for a staggering £247,000. Despite this, they separated after 28 years of marriage – presumably the house was not the problem. In 1879 Corbett bought, and vastly improved, St Andrew's House. He renamed it the Raven Hotel, after the raven on the Corbett family's coat of arms (from the French for raven, 'le corbeau'... which sounds a bit like 'Corbett').

To some extent, the use of ice (▶ Walk 6) and, later, refrigeration, as a means of preserving meats and other foods contributed to the decline of Droitwich's salt production, which ceased in 1922. The Worcestershire Brine Baths Hotel on St Andrew's Road is, in its own way, 'spectacular' for it has been shut for roughly two decades. The site is in the hands of the same people who own the Raven Hotel (just across the way) and Château Impney. It may have been flattened or put to some use, at least, by the time you do this walk.

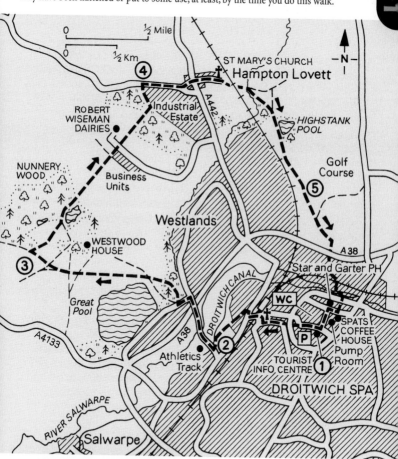

Walk 11 **Directions**

① Begin at the tourist information centre. Go along **Victoria Square**. Cross Heritage Way, noting the especially ugly **Orchard House**

(surely 1960s?) on the corner, into **Ombersley Street East**. When it bends go straight on, passing the magistrates' court (not much better). After an underpass proceed to **St Nicholas's Church**. Go round the churchyard to take another underpass. Turn left. Take the road over the railway to a mini-roundabout, filtering right to go through a third underpass. Walk for 65yds (60m) to a fence corner, near a lamppost. Turn left. In 30yds (27m) turn right. At the bottom of this cul-de-sac, **Westmead Close**, turn left. Soon take **Ledwych Close**, on the right. At the canal you are effectively out of Droitwich Spa.

② Turn left. At the bridge turn right, passing sundry sporty places. Turn left just beyond the A38 bridge. In 110yds (100m) reach the **Westwood House** slip road. Facing some allotments, take a kissing gate to the left. Beyond this woodland go straight across several fields. Within 500yds (457m) of the second driveway is a junction.

③ Turn sharply right. Electric fencing shepherds you between paddocks before you veer left to walk briefly through **Nunnery Wood**. Aim for two gateposts beside a solitary, squat tree. Keep straight on for ½ mile (800m), beside the big dairy on the left, then curving left past an industrial estate to reach **Doverdale Lane**.

④ Turn right along the lane. Just before a '30' speed-limit sign, fork left. Cross the A442. Walk through the hamlet of **Hampton Lovett** to **St Mary's Church**. (It is asymmetrical, having a curved Norman column on its left side.) Take the meadow path under the

railway. In 140yds (128m), at a footbridge, bear right, along a field edge. Keep following this general line for over ½ mile (800m), walking in the trees beside **Highstank Pool** when the wire fence allows. Then a clear track leads to young evergreens shielding a golf tee.

⑤ Cross a vast field, then aim slightly left to a metal gate. Follow the road under the **A38** into a housing estate. Find a path running between Nos 49 and 53 (51 is hidden). Go through two kissing gates flanking the level crossing. Turn left to pass the **Gardeners Arms**. In 20yds (18m) turn right over the River Salwarpe, into **Vines Park**. Veer left to cross the **Droitwich Canal**. Over the B4090, follow **Gurney Lane** to **High Street** – in front of you is **Spats Coffee House**. Turn right, passing **Tower Hill**, then left into **St Andrew's Street** and thence to the start of the walk.

Sights and Smells of Worcester City

The city of Worcester is known for Sir Edward Elgar, its battle, its sauce, its porcelain and its racecourse; but what of its largely unsung hero?

•DISTANCE•	2½ miles (4km)
•MINIMUM TIME•	1hr 30min
•ASCENT / GRADIENT•	Negligible
•LEVEL OF DIFFICULTY•	
•PATHS•	City streets and tarmac riverside path
•LANDSCAPE•	Urban with riverside
•SUGGESTED MAP•	aqua3 OS Explorer 204 Worcester & Droitwich Spa
•START / FINISH•	Grid reference: SO 846548
•DOG FRIENDLINESS•	Not dog friendly (except short stretch by river)
•PARKING•	Long-stay pay-and-display car parks at New Road, Tybridge Street and Croft Road (and elsewhere)
•PUBLIC TOILETS•	Near start at Croft Road and bus station; several elsewhere

BACKGROUND TO THE WALK

The development of Lea & Perrins' Worcester Sauce was largely accidental. The story goes that the two chemists, who ran a store between Broad Street and Bank Street (just off High Street), were asked to make up a recipe brought back from abroad in the 1820s. This they did, making an extra jar for themselves. Finding it excessively hot, they put the jar aside. Some years later they stumbled upon it and, quite bravely, sipped it – eureka! It had mellowed to a pleasant piquancy. The secrecy surrounding the recipe is (apparently) retained, eccentrically but effectively, firstly by employing any given worker only on part of the process, and secondly by giving the ingredients meaningless code names. HP Foods, which is now owned by French giant Danone, bought the business back in 1930. It has since gone on to achieve worldwide brand status.

New Street

Keep your eyes directed at least 10ft (3m) off the ground and New Street – actually rather old – is a visual feast. New Street wasn't even new then – it had been Glover Street. In the late 18th century many merchants migrated from here, making their houses tenements and workshops. The merchants left partly because of the stench. Nowadays the most likely smell wafting down New Street is fast food. An 1832 report said of The Shambles that 'filth of all description remains until it is perfectly alive', and in 1846 another said that in parts of Worcester 'pools of liquid filth perpetually stagnate the surface.' The juxtaposition of slaughterhouses and their waste shouldn't be forgotten. Big-time disease was inevitable.

Sir Charles Hastings

Charles Hastings was a brilliant youth. He attended anatomy school in London when 16, became house surgeon to Worcester Infirmary aged 18, went to Edinburgh University aged 21, and returned to Worcester Infirmary. (He declined a professorship at Edinburgh.) Ahead of his time, Hastings believed that the state should be responsible for the health of its public. He conducted much research into what nowadays would be called 'occupational health' – of local porcelain workers, glovers, and saltworkers, for example – and founded the Provincial Medical and Surgical Association. Twenty-four years later, with Hastings still at the helm, legislation formally established this body as the British Medical Association, which still oversees the work of medical practitioners today. It is said that he attended every case during the three cholera outbreaks in 1832, 1849 and 1853.

A True Philanthropist

In 1854 Dr Hastings put much of his own money into innovative 'modern dwellings' (long-demolished, off Copenhagen Street) for artisans. He at least had the satisfaction of seeing the local death rate fall by 45 per cent in a decade. However, he still had a fight on his hands to persuade the city council to provide clean water. Amazingly, legislation compelling local councils to do this did not reach the statute books until 1872.

He benefitted the people of Worcester in several other ways too, such as by founding a natural history museum in the city. His grave lies in Worcester's Astwood Cemetery. When he died in 1866, aged 72, Sir Charles Hastings was Worcester's most lauded citizen; at that time Edward Elgar was only nine years old. One could argue as to which brought about the greater benefit to Worcester city.

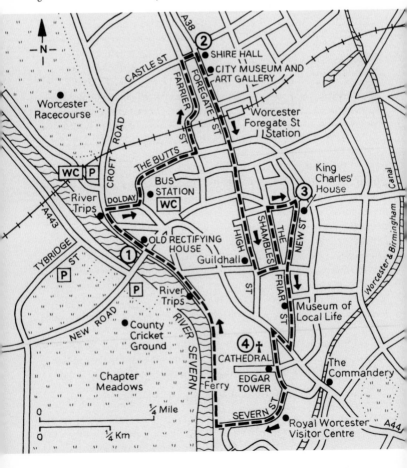

Walk 12 Directions

① The described route begins at the city side of the road bridge, but you can pick it up anywhere – at The Commandery or the Guildhall, for example – depending on where you have parked. Turn left, along **North Parade**, passing the **Old Rectifying House** (wine bar). Turn right up **Dolday**, then left, in front of the bus station, along **The Butts**. Turn left along **Farrier Street**, right into **Castle Street**, reaching the northern extremity of the route at its junction with **Foregate Street**.

> **WHAT TO LOOK FOR** ℹ️
>
> **Elgar's statue** is at the bottom of High Street (in which his father had a shop). The architectural historian Nikolaus Pevsner, writing in his *Buildings of England* in 1968, described the then new central city development around High Street as 'hara-kiri by the city, not murder by the architects.' In New Street, **King Charles' House** is where the young man stayed during the Battle of Worcester in 1651.

② Go right along Foregate Street, passing the Shire Hall and the City Museum and Art Gallery, continuing along **The Cross** and into the pedestrianised area called **High Street**. Turn left into **Pump Street**. (Elgar's statue stands close to his father's piano shop, at the southern end of High Street.) Turn left again, into **The Shambles**. At a junction turn right into **Mealcheapen Street**. Another right turn and you are in **New Street** (which later becomes Friar Street).

③ Head down this partial time-warp as slowly as you can, for a dual carriageway (**College Street**) awaits you at the end. Turn right, then cross over carefully, to visit the **cathedral**.

④ Leave the cathedral along **College Precincts** to the fortified gateway known as **Edgar Tower**. (It is named after the 10th-century King Edgar, but was actually built in the 14th century. Go through this gateway to see College Green.) Continue, along what is now **Severn Street** which, unsurprisingly, leads to the River Severn. Turn right, to complete your circuit, by following **Kleve Walk**, a leafy waterside avenue; this section floods at some time most winters, and the cricket ground opposite was under several feet of water in 2000.

> **WHERE TO EAT AND DRINK**
>
> Options abound – the 'civic' ones are relatively unusual. Try the **Balcony Café** at the partly baroque, partly Tudor City Museum and Art Gallery in Foregate Street; built in 1896 (and then named, dully, the Victoria Institute), it's a delightfully airy place to sit for lunch, a snack, or tea and scones. Or try the **Assembly Rooms** restaurant, up on the second floor of the Italianate Guildhall.

> **WHILE YOU'RE THERE** ℹ️
>
> For a studied insight into the city's history, go on a **guided walk** (weekdays only) with a Green Badge Guide. **The Commandery** is Worcester's English Civil War museum – the Royalists headquartered here. History within living memory is easily recalled at the **Museum of Local Life** (in Friar Street). **River trips** depart from both North Quay and South Quay. There's a ferry too, from behind the cathedral to Chapter Meadows. The **Royal Worcester Visitor Centre** is open daily; bookable factory tours run Monday to Friday (except during shutdowns).

Kingsford Country Park and Villages

A Worcestershire backwater that once knew busier times.

•DISTANCE•	5½ miles (8.8km)
•MINIMUM TIME•	2hrs 30min
•ASCENT / GRADIENT•	410ft (125m)
•LEVEL OF DIFFICULTY•	
•PATHS•	Forest rides, meadows, minor roads, village streets, canal tow path, 9 stiles
•LANDSCAPE•	Mostly pastures and woodland in rolling countryside
•SUGGESTED MAP•	aqua3 OS Explorer 218 Wyre Forest & Kidderminster or 219 Wolverhampton & Dudley
•START / FINISH•	Grid reference: SO 835820
•DOG FRIENDLINESS•	Much fun in woods but horses and sheep elsewhere
•PARKING•	Blakeshall Lane car park, Kingsford Country Park
•PUBLIC TOILETS•	None on route

BACKGROUND TO THE WALK

On this and other walks you may come across dense spindley woodland that somehow 'doesn't look right'. Such areas of trees may be to the oak what a pile of stones is to an old church: a ruin. The occurrence of the word 'coppice' on a map – Solcum Coppice, Gloucester Coppice – often indicates a woodland of historical importance to the local economy. With its proximity to the industries of the West Midlands, local charcoal production (especially in the Wyre Forest) was considerable.

Invention or Discovery?

Is charcoal an invention or a discovery? Probably it was 'discovered' by accident, and its subsequent uses were invented. It is wood that has been incompletely burned (in a controlled way) by being deprived of much of the oxygen that would otherwise render it a pile of ashes. Woods used for charcoal-making include hazel – a favourite because of its prolific re-growth – ash, oak and alder buckthorn, among others.

A Slow Process

The raw material was cut and left to dry or 'season' for several months before use. This, together with how well and for how long the 'kiln' was burning, were key factors in determining the yield – 15–25 per cent was good, and 30 per cent exceptional. The kiln was a temporary structure, essentially a mound or dome of logs carefully constructed around a central airway, the whole being covered with turf, ideal since the roots of the grass bound the soil together tightly, and the turfs were easier to handle than soil on its own. Turf would also be used to cover the airway once a fire had been established at the core. It could take several days to complete the charcoal-making process. Of course, much of the weight lost is evaporated moisture. When re-ignited, it burns with an intensity capable of smelting metal, forging iron, and making glass, as well as blackening your burger. Gunpowder is concocted from three ingredients – charcoal, sulphur and saltpetre (potassium nitrate). Only when the coal derivative, coke, was introduced was charcoal superseded as an intensive heat source. (Coke later gave way to oil and gas, which also have the advantage of being easier to control.)

Charcoal in the 21st Century

Don't think that your summertime barbeques are necessarily being fuelled by British-grown trees, for in all probability they aren't. Approximately 95 per cent of the charcoal sold in Britain is imported, a statistic that upsets environmentalists greatly, since much of it is sourced from the notoriously unsustained tropical rain forests. The British countryside has a vast stock of growing wood that could be managed in a sustainable way, that is, harvested cyclically, without reducing the total tree stock, but the high income expectation of labour makes it an uneconomic proposition. Or does it? At the last count the BioRegional Charcoal Company, a marketing co-operative, had over 40 members.

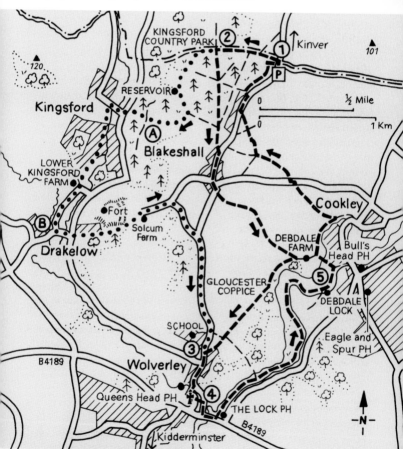

Walk 13 Directions

① Take the track inside the northern edge of the country park for 550yds (503m), to a point about 50yds (46m) beyond the end of the extensive garden. To the left is a wide glade, falling gently; ahead rises the woodland track (Walk 14).

Walk 13

② Turn left, down the ride. In 275yds (251m), at a five-way junction, go ahead (not along a slight right fork). Join a farm track. At a road turn right, through **Blakeshall**. After 300yds (274m), at a right-hand bend near power lines, take a stile into a muddy and brick-strewn field. Keep a hedge on your right, following yellow waymarkers into a small valley. Reach, but don't go through, a seven-bar metal gate before **Debdale Farm**. Turn sharply to the right, uphill, following a vague track. Enter **Gloucester Coppice** at a gate and broken stile. Follow this track, soon more defined, all the way to the southern end of **Blakeshall Lane** (where Walk 14 rejoins).

③ Turn left, descending through the street called **The Holloway**, into Wolverley. After the village stores take the second footbridge on the right. Reach the **Church of St John the Baptist** by zig-zagging up the concreted footpath through a deep cutting. Leave the churchyard to the left, by modern steps. Go down the meadow opposite (with a fingerpost) to a minor road.

④ Turn right. At the **B4189** turn left. In front of **The Lock** public house turn left, along the tow path. After about 1¼ miles (2km) is **Debdale Lock**, partly hewn into the rock. Some 220yds (201m) further, just before the steel wheel factory, is a stile.

⑤ Turn left here along a track. (Alternatively continue for 150yds/137m for refreshments in Cookley.) At a T-junction after a coniferous avenue turn right on a broad gravel track. After about 440yds (402m) turn left (waymarker), up some new wooden steps surfaced with scalpings, into trees. Go up the left-hand edge of one field and the centre of another to a road. Turn left for just 15yds (14m), then right. Some 400yds (366m) along this hedged lane take the yellow option to the right (to reduce road walking). At the next stile wiggle left then right. Proceed straight ahead at a junction to the road. Turn right. In 150yds (137m) walk round the wooden barrier to re-enter the country park. Two paths run parallel to the road – both lead back to the car park.

A Longer Walk in Kingsford Country Park

This extension, looping through a country park, includes two short sections of the Worcestershire Way.
See map and information panel for Walk 13

•DISTANCE•	7¼ miles (11.7km)
•MINIMUM TIME•	3hrs
•ASCENT / GRADIENT•	560ft (170m) ▲ ▲ ▲
•LEVEL OF DIFFICULTY•	👫 👫 👫

Walk 14 Directions (Walk 13 option)

At Point ② continue for 160yds (146m) to the county border and the sign: 'Worcestershire Way, Staffordshire Way, North Worcestershire Path'. Turn left down this good track, skirting round to the left of the fenced-off covered reservoir, and using the track below it (follow waymarkers). After 160yds (146m) you reach a point where you have three choices. Do not take the left fork, but take the nearer, lower of two options to the right, that is, through a single-bar gate, passing a bench 30yds (27m) beyond it, and not beside hurdle-style fencing above it. Go along here for 425yds (389m) to reach a T-junction, Point Ⓐ.

Here, do not turn left along the Worcestershire Way, but turn right for just 20yds (18m) then left, on a muddy path running through pines and silver birch. Reach a road junction within 200yds (183m) and go down the stem of the T-junction. Within 160yds (146m) take the waymarked path left, opposite the house, 'Saddlebrook Kingsford'. This green band improves to become a metalled road. Turn right, passing **Lower Kingsford Farm**, to reach a T-junction, Point Ⓑ.

Here turn left, crossing over to the pavement set back from the road. At the next T-junction cross the road and go straight on, along a works access road, to reach a gate into woods. Ascend gently. Beside a house with intricate fencing, join a lane that goes straight ahead. At the next junction turn right, away from the Worcestershire Way, following this minor road (becoming **Blakeshall Lane**) towards Wolverley. Shortly before you reach the village pass **Wolverley High School,** then rejoin Walk 13.

WHILE YOU'RE THERE ⓘ

If you visit the **Bodenham Arboretum and Earth Centre**, be sure to allow enough time to do justice to its 134 acres (54ha) and its 2,500 or so tree species. The arboretum is open daily from April through to mid-November, and at weekends for the rest of the year. Dogs on leads are welcome in the grounds. The 'lavender tunnel' is particularly striking in the late spring.

Walk 15

Upton upon Severn

An easy walk to a black-and-white village, returning by the river.

•**DISTANCE**•	5¾ miles (9.2km)
•**MINIMUM TIME**•	2hrs 30min
•**ASCENT / GRADIENT**•	80ft (25m) ▲ ▲ ▲
•**LEVEL OF DIFFICULTY**•	🚶 🚶 🚶
•**PATHS**•	Meadows, lanes, tracks, village streets, riverside, 9 stiles
•**LANDSCAPE**•	Low-lying meadows, fruit farms, villages, small town
•**SUGGESTED MAP**•	aqua3 OS Explorer 190 Malvern Hills & Bredon Hill
•**START / FINISH**•	Grid reference: SO 850402
•**DOG FRIENDLINESS**•	Some opportunities for trustworthy dogs to be off leads
•**PARKING**•	Free car park opposite Church of St Peter and St Paul
•**PUBLIC TOILETS**•	In town centre

Walk 15 **Directions**

Begin away from Upton, along the **A4104**. The 'new' Church of St Peter and St Paul was built in 1878–9 in a neo-Gothic style. Shortly take the old road right, skirting sports fields. Less than 50yds (46m) before this rejoins the A4104, turn right again. At the bend take stiles on the right. Near the field end go left, through a plantation. At a sunken lane turn left, to houses and a street.

Walk beside a playing field, then turn right, passing a children's play area. Take the second public footpath on the right, initially beside ash trees, later through an orchard. Cross a road, going down another orchard row, admiring the Discovery apples and Czar plums of **Clive's Fruit Farm**. At the end move left to cross the old railway track by wooden steps. (In autumn you should feel some empathy for the notorious 'leaves on the line' problem.) Follow a sunken lane. Turn left at a road. At a junction

turn right, soon taking a gravel driveway left between two bridges. Go right of the house to a stile beyond its sheds. Pass some hazel coppice on the right. A huge conifer marks **Hanley Castle**'s site.

The castle that stood here was, in the 13th century, part of the Earl of Gloucester's estate. It was mostly demolished, when already a ruin, at the time of Henry VIII, but some residual stone was later used to repair Upton's bridge.

At the next stile turn right to a gate with a concealed side stile and a second stile beyond it. Just through the latter on the left is an iron kissing gate. Take the left-hand field edge. Enter the churchyard, ignoring waymarkers.

The chunk of brickwork – the central tower, the north chapel, and the chancel – was added in 1674, whereas the stonework is largely 14th-century. Near by, the timber frames of the almshouses are from 1600, but they were rebuilt in the early 19th century. The school has been added to, piecemeal, with varying degrees of architectural sense, since its foundation in 1544.

Walk down the village street to the **B4211**. Turn right along the pavement for 220yds (201m). Cross at the cross. **Quay Lane** leads to the river. Turn right, soon edging a vast arable field.

The craftsmen of Upton's boatbuilders, cartwrights and the like are believed to have aided the Parliamentarians in their preparations for the Battle of Worcester in 1651 (► Walk 20). They built two pontoons, which were hauled by the Parliamentary army from Upton to the Teme–Severn confluence, They used these two 'bridges of boats' to cross each river, giving them a great strategic advantage. Close to the river, the tower of Upton's old church, built on a 13th-century base, was the scene of a skirmish a few days before the decisive battle. The remainder of the church was demolished in 1937; a 14th-century effigy and several memorials were transferred to the new church.

After a long ½ mile (800m) rejoin the B4211's pavement. Go under **Upton Bridge**, past its predecessor's site and three pubs.

At Upton the River Severn has only 36ft (11m) to fall to the sea. After the heavy rains of some recent winters the town has been dubbed 'Upton under Severn'. The arguments on flood control will never cease, although not building on a flood plain would seem a natural starting point. (The back page of the town's visitor directory carries an advertisement for flood damage repair.) Up in the Welsh mountains and not far from the slopes of Pumlumon, where the River Severn rises, is Llyn Clywedog Reservoir. It was built in the 1960s to control the flow of the river, providing extra water in periods of drought and preventing flooding downriver but, even boasting the highest mass concrete dam in Britain, it can only hold so much.

Keep beside the river on a road. A gate leads on to **Upton Hams**. After a short ½ mile (800m), at a fishery sign, turn right. A kissing gate gives on to a vehicular track. At the first tarmac road go straight ahead. At the crossroads turn right into **School Lane**, all the way to the town centre. (Turn right for the tourist information centre in High Street.) If you learn nothing else from this walk, please remember that the 1850 Roman Catholic Chapel of St Joseph in School Lane was built by a C Hansom, the brother of taxi cab designer Joseph Hansom, and that the racing driver Nigel Mansell was born in Upton upon Severn on 8 August 1953. Turn left along **Old Street** to return to your car.

Walk 16

Ombersley and Holt Fleet

Explore an estate park and the banks of the River Severn.

•DISTANCE•	5¾ miles (9.2km)
•MINIMUM TIME•	2hrs 30min
•ASCENT / GRADIENT•	200ft (61m)
•LEVEL OF DIFFICULTY•	
•PATHS•	Riverside paths, field paths and tracks, village street, 9 stiles
•LANDSCAPE•	Estate parkland, riverside meadows and general farmland
•SUGGESTED MAP•	aqua3 OS Explorer 204 Worcester & Droitwich Spa
•START / FINISH•	Grid reference: SO 845630
•DOG FRIENDLINESS•	Few off-lead opportunities unless very obedient
•PARKING•	Towards southern end of road through Ombersley on eastern side (southbound exit from village)
•PUBLIC TOILETS•	None on route

BACKGROUND TO THE WALK

Ombersley must have been awful before the bypass, but now it verges on the tranquil. Ombersley Court was built in the 1720s. Apparently it has a superb interior, but the nearest you'll get to even a reasonable view of it is at the far end of the churchyard (beside a grim memorial tree). Sited on the Ombersley Park Estate, St Andrew's Church was built 100 years after Ombersley Court, but in the decorated style of the early 14th century, presumably to reflect the fragment of the original church (now a mausoleum) behind it.

Silence of the Owls

Along the river towards Holt Bridge, to your right (and left also) is a classic stretch of woodland, adorning the steep slopes of the great River Severn's flood plain. If you were to walk along here at dusk you could hope to see an owl, possibly even a barn owl, but you probably wouldn't. A survey conducted in Worcestershire in 1932 found 184 breeding pairs of barn owls, but a similar survey in 1985 found just 32. There were numerous reasons for its decline. Part of the blame is apportioned to the grubbing out of the hedgerows, thereby removing a good habitat for small mammals. However, much is apportioned to intensive agriculture's use of pesticides, moving along the food chain so that, by the time a barn owl has eaten 100 or so slightly contaminated but well mammals (mice, shrews, voles), the cumulative dosage of pesticide is fatal.

The goal of the Worcestershire Barn Owl Society (WBOS) is to reverse the trend, partly by breeding barn owls and releasing them in carefully chosen locations. Barn owls are quite happy in tree hollows but, no, they rarely approve of barn conversions. The WBOS builds and erects nest boxes in strategic places to compensate for the loss – you can even buy or sponsor one. Like other owls, the barn owl flies silently, a useful hunting trick, achieved by having soft tips to its wing feathers – these tips effectively deaden any airflow noise.

Holt Fleet

The bridge at Holt Fleet replaced a ferry. It was the last in Worcestershire to cease taking tolls. (In Herefordshire tolls are still taken at the 1802 Whitney Bridge, near Walk 47.) Such was the belief in a German invasion that mines were laid under the Holt Fleet Bridge during the Second World War. The Holt Fleet Inn was built well before the bridge, and benefited greatly from the day-tripper business, being the northern terminus for paddle steamer trips from Worcester, about 7 miles (11.3km) to the south. These trips ran until the 1930s. In contrast, the Wharf Inn, on the east bank, marks the site of a coal wharf. Holt Lock, a little way upstream, was completed in 1844.

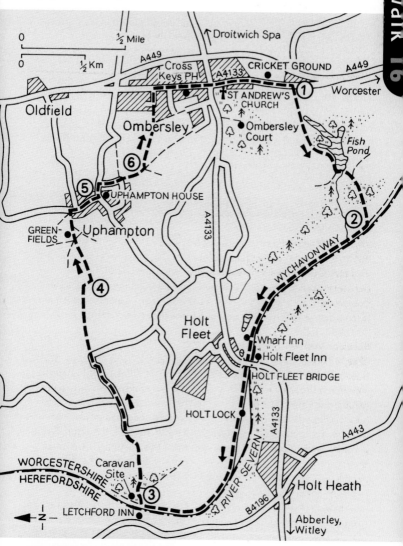

Walk 16 Directions

① To the south of the village, and beyond the **cricket ground**, take a path on the right. This is the

Wychavon Way. Briefly in trees, walk across a meadow to a stile beside a willow. Go along the left-hand field edge, and briefly by the water's edge. At the corner of the fish pond a waymarker leads out to

Walk 16

a track. Turn left, following this track right in 80yds (73m). It becomes a sunken path through delicious woodland. Cross a meadow to the river.

② Turn right. In a short mile (1.6km) you'll pass two fishing pools to reach **Holt Fleet Bridge**. Go under this, continuing for about the same distance, passing the staffed **Holt Lock**. When opposite the **Letchford Inn** you'll come to a riverside stile.

③ Don't go over this stile; instead, turn right. In the field corner join the access road. At a junction go straight ahead on the public road. In 650yds (594m), at a right-hand bend, keep this line by moving left, on to a farm track. The large area on the right was formerly an orchard, but it has gone completely. It's over ¼ mile (400m) to the top of

this field. When you are 30yds (27m) before a rusty shed, turn right. Now, in about 75yds (69m), go left, over a stile.

④ What could be a golf course fairway turns out to be an enormous garden. Aim to pass to the right of the house, by a children's wooden watchtower. Cross the gravel in front of the house, **Greenfields**, to go down its private driveway. Turn right for 275yds (251m), passing several black-and-white houses, to a T-junction – **Uphampton House** is in front of you.

⑤ Turn left for 110yds (100m), then turn right, uphill. In 150yds (137m) don't bend right but go straight ahead, on a shingly track. About 220yds (201m) further, the main track bends right, a rough track goes ahead and a public footpath goes half left.

⑥ Take the public footpath option, along a field edge. Continue through a small area of market garden, reaching a cul-de-sac. Shortly turn right, along the village street. There are many houses to look at, the churches of St Andrew (current and former), and several points of refreshment to delay your return to your car.

Hartlebury Common and Stourport-on-Severn

Cut through a Georgian 'new town' before striding out across a common.

•DISTANCE•	3¼ miles (5.3km)
•MINIMUM TIME•	1hr 30min
•ASCENT / GRADIENT•	328ft (100m) ▲ ▲ ▲
•LEVEL OF DIFFICULTY•	🚶🚶 🚶🚶 🚶🚶
•PATHS•	Tow path, tracks, good paths, some streets
•LANDSCAPE•	Urban, watery, and common with extensive views
•SUGGESTED MAP•	aqua3 OS Explorer 218 Wyre Forest & Kidderminster or 219 Wolverhampton & Dudley
•START / FINISH•	Grid reference: SO 820704
•DOG FRIENDLINESS•	Good on common and tow path, not much fun in town
•PARKING•	Worcester Road car park on A4025 (poorly signed; black-and-white height restriction bar spans narrow entrance)
•PUBLIC TOILETS•	None on route

BACKGROUND TO THE WALK

You will understand the rise and fall of Stourport-on-Severn if you look at a map of England. The infrastructural advantage realised by the opening of the Staffordshire and Worcestershire Canal was to link the River Severn with the Rivers Trent and Mersey.

Horse Power, Canal Power

Canals were conceived when road transport was not only uncomfortable for passengers but also extremely slow for goods, and railways had yet to be invented. Roads were in a poor condition, invariably worsened by the winter months. River transport was, at least, an option along the Severn. (In comparison, Herefordshire's River Wye was usually too low in the summer months to give sufficient draught to even a small sailing barge.) A horse and cart could carry perhaps 300lb (136kg). Along a canal tow path, a horse could haul a barge carrying a vastly greater burden – up to 50 tons (50,679kg), a more than 300-fold weight advantage. Although the horse moved slowly, it is easy to see how those with money to invest fashionably threw it at all manner of canal projects (► Walks 26 and 27). For Joe Public the main outcome was cheaper coal.

Steam Horse

In 1771, when the Staffordshire and Worcestershire Canal opened, Stourport grew up, becoming perhaps what we would call a 'new town'. Apart from the barge and boat building, foundries and carpet factories, for example, were opened too. After just four decades, trade was hit by the new Worcester and Birmingham Canal, which had itself been 24 years in the making (► Walk 3). Railway proliferation sent Stourport into further decline.

When the canals were nationalised in 1948, the days of commercial canal activity were already numbered. In the case of the Worcester and Birmingham Canal, the last two companies to use the canal regularly stopped in the early 1960s; they were Worcester's Royal

Porcelain (for coal) and Cadbury's of Bournville (for chocolate crumb). The commercial activity seen on the canal nowadays is of a totally different sort – canal-boat cruising is an enormously popular holiday choice.

Birth of the Family Narrow Boat

In a sense we have the railways to thank for canal-boat holidays. Trains were to prove the undoing of the canals (as lorries were to prove the undoing of the railways), but the initial response by the canal operators was to cut prices, and this meant cutting costs. Labour was not in short supply, so wages for boatmen were cut; their response, since so much of their time was spent on the water anyway, was to shed the burden of rent-paying by bringing their families on board their barges – the family narrow boat was born.

Walk 17 Directions

① Cross the **A4025**. Turn left for just 25yds (23m) to take a footpath. Strike across this bottom part of **Hartlebury Common**: you'll see some buildings in the far distance. Veer right, through spindly silver birches, to find a sandy track at the back of some houses with scruffy gardens. At a modern housing estate join the tarmac briefly, aiming for a dirt track beyond the

second 'Britannia Gardens' sign and
in front of **Globe House**. Shortly
turn left down a tarmac footpath,
initially with wooden paling on the
left, to the river.

② Turn right. In 650yds (594m)
you'll reach a lock and Stourport's
canal basins. You'll probably want
to spend some time exploring here.
However, the route is neither across
the two-plank walkway at the upper
lock gate, nor the upper brick
bridge with timber and metal
railings; instead take the neat brick-
paved path to circumnavigate the
boarded-up **Tontine** public house.
Now skirt the **Upper Basin**, passing
the **Severn Valley Boat Centre**.
Across **York Street** join the tow
path. Follow this for a little under
¾ mile (1.2km), leaving it at the
Bird in Hand, before a defunct
brick railway bridge.

③ Go down **Holly Road**, then half
left into **Mill Road**, passing under
the railway then over the River
Stour to the **B4193**. Cross and go to
the left of Myday Windows to take
a narrow, sandy, uphill path back on
to the common. Soon, at a fork, go

left, keeping in this direction as the
ground levels. Less than 50 paces
after joining a motor vehicle track
reach the unpainted trig point.

④ Now retrace those 50 paces and
go a further 30yds (27m), passing a
wooden waymarker, to a junction.
Here turn left, away from the car
park. In just 40yds (37m) take the
right fork, then in 100yds (91m)
take a left fork (not straight on). At
the corner of a conifer plantation,
275yds further (251m), turn right.
After 110yds (100m) turn left, then
in 220yds (201m), just after the far
end of the plantation, enjoy views
to the west. Now 65yds (60m)
beyond this viewpoint take the right
option at a subtle fork. Go forward
on this for another 250yds (229m),
until an opening. Here step very
carefully over a pair of exposed
and disused (and not actually
hazardous) pipes. Follow the sandy
track slanting downhill for (110yds)
100m, then swing right, now
making a beeline for the car park.

Great Witley Circuit: a Sneeze in the Trees

A mostly woodland walk up and down some of Worcestershire's lesser-known hills.

•DISTANCE•	4¾ miles (7.7km)
•MINIMUM TIME•	2hrs 45min
•ASCENT / GRADIENT•	1,150ft (350m) ▲▲▲
•LEVEL OF DIFFICULTY•	🏃🏃🏃
•PATHS•	Woodland paths, field paths, tracks, 9 stiles
•LANDSCAPE•	Wooded hills and farmed valleys
•SUGGESTED MAP•	aqua3 OS Explorer 204 Worcester & Droitwich Spa
•START / FINISH•	Grid reference: SO 752662
•DOG FRIENDLINESS•	Will be driven wild by geese! Running in woods but leads needed over grazing land
•PARKING•	Large car park of Hundred House Hotel (as a courtesy please phone beforehand, tel 01299 896888)
•PUBLIC TOILETS•	None on route

BACKGROUND TO THE WALK

What sort of walker are you – 'any weather' or 'fair weather'? Or are you a 'low pollen count walker', suffering from hay fever? Grasses are the most common cause, but allergy is by no means confined to these – just about any pollen can produce allergenic reactions. Between 10 per cent and 35 per cent of us suffer from 'pollinosis' (allergy to pollen), but these reactions may be species-specific. In addition, some species of tree seem to have more potent pollen than others, birch in particular. Pollen is typically released from grasses from May to August, oilseed rape from April to June, and stinging nettles from May to mid-September. These are all good reasons for getting out walking in the winter, but if you are afflicted in January it could be pollen from alder or hazel, and in March it could be birch. Studies show that the season for birch pollen has shifted to five days earlier every decade over the past 30 years, a clear indication of global warming. Put that way it may not seem much, but it's actually half a month.

Bronchitis

The National Pollen Research Unit (NPRU), at University College, Worcester, is at the forefront of the science of 'aerobiology'. Supplying pollen forecasts is just one of the NPRU's diverse activities; others include studying changes in pollen seasons in relation to climate change, and studying asthma in relation to fungi and house-dust mites in homes. The Unit is currently undertaking a local three-year study (2003–6) into chronic bronchitis – properly, chronic obstructive pulmonary disease (COPD). It is caused primarily by smoking, but there are other, secondary factors at work – this must be the case, because in some southern European countries people smoke more but there is less COPD. The finger of suspicion is pointed at Britain's higher humidity. The research is focused on whether or not (and if so, how) mists and fogs can increase the likelihood of this illness occurring.

Happy Geese

From early spring until mid-December the lane around Walsgrove Farm is awash with geese – about 3,500 of them. This is just another of the diverse activities you can come across in the back lanes of Worcestershire and Herefordshire. They are prepared for sale using an on-site 'low throughput processing unit'. Until then, these free-range birds are allowed to range very freely. Nearly all are destined for the Christmas table, primarily through butchers and retailers, but you can buy one at the farm gate too.

Walk 18

Walk 18 Directions

① Cross the **A451** with great care. Through an opening, strike sharply right, aiming for the hedge end beside the last house. Step over the fence then turn left on this lane. Walk for ½ mile (800m) along here, soon passing firstly **Walsgrove Farm** and secondly (most of the year) thousands of strutting, wailing geese. Do not turn right up a lane but go half right, taking the path that becomes a beautiful avenue of conifers, to the top of **Woodbury Hill**. At a marker post go straight over on a narrower track. In 130yds (119m) reach a farm track above **Lippetts Farm**.

② Turn right, descending. At a hairpin bend, aim away from the farm to walk along the inside edge of a wood. Skirt to the left of the buildings at **Birch Berrow**, resuming on a service road. As this goes up, right, to an exercise ring for horses, take the right-hand of two gates. Go steeply down, taking a stile into thick pines. Very soon, over another stile, turn right along the tarmac road for 100yds (91m), so that you are past 1 Hillside Cottages, not before it.

③ Turn right again, back uphill. Continue north for nearly 1 mile (1.6km), over several stiles, walking mostly in trees but later enjoying fine views westwards. Then, on top of **Walsgrove Hill**, you'll see the elaborate and magnificent clock tower (1883) of Abberley Hall. Now go steeply down this meadow, to take a stile into a lane. Turn right for 80yds (73m) to the **B4203**.

④ Cross carefully. Turn left, along the verge. Take the driveway to **Abberley Hall School**. Leave the driveway as it swings right, keeping this direction close to the clock tower and all the way, on a track, to the **A443**. Take the road opposite, 'Wynniatts Way', up to the brow of the hill.

⑤ Turn right. In about 400yds (366m) reach a bright **trig point**. Walk along the ridge path a further 650yds (594m) to a Worcestershire Way sign at a path junction, just beyond which are four trees growing in a line across the path. (Walk 19 rejoins here.)

⑥ Take the path down to the right, initially quite steeply then contouring as it veers right, later descending again. Emerge from the woods over a stile to walk down two large fields, meeting the road beside the **Hundred House Hotel**.

WHAT TO LOOK FOR ⓘ

The **Hundred House Hotel** was once a collecting centre for tithes from the local area's districts or 'hundreds'. Today's hotel has an enclosed beer garden to the side and an extensive menu. Children are welcome but dogs are only allowed in the garden. On Walk 19 the **Manor Arms at Abberley** has a roadside terrace.

WHILE YOU'RE THERE ⓘ

Despite its size, **Witley Court**, 1¼ miles (2km) south east of Great Witley, is unseen on the walk itself. No public footpaths go near Witley Court, and the road that serves it (and the church) is unadopted. But do make an effort to visit this stunning building. The Court's 'in-your-face' architecture, mostly Victorian, is just stunning. Only the skeleton remains, since its flesh was burned by a fire in 1937. English Heritage describe it as their number one ruin. Adjacent to Witley Court, **St Michael's Church** is also worth a visit.

Abberley Village and Abberley Hill

A detour through Abberley Village and back through hilly woodland.
See map and information panel for Walk 18

•DISTANCE•	7¾ miles (12.5km)
•MINIMUM TIME•	4hrs 15min
•ASCENT / GRADIENT•	1,540ft (469m) ▲▲▲
•LEVEL OF DIFFICULTY•	🚶🚶 🚶🚶 🚶🚶

Walk 19 Directions
(Walk 18 option)

At Point ⑤ on Walk 18 keep on the road, descending steeply for 180yds (165m). Follow the Worcestershire Way fingerpost down some wooden steps. (The tree roots lower down are treacherous when wet.) Take a stile out of the woods, and more stiles across meadows down to **The Village**, Abberley, Point Ⓐ.

The focal point here is the old church, or perhaps the pub opposite. Dedicated to St Michael, only the Norman chancel remains fully intact. A door and sturdy glass panelling divide it from the remainder, now ruins and exposed to the elements. Abberley's 'new' church is dedicated to St Mary. It lies a couple of minutes' walk from the village. Although 13th-century in style, it was built a mere 150 years ago and largely rebuilt after a fire in 1876.

Turn left, passing the **Manor Arms at Abberley** pub. Ignore the first two fingerposts on the left but take the third, a few paces past a driveway. Leave this meadow by a stile, on to a track heading straight for a cottage. Just before its garage there's a signposted path to the left, past the cottage's garden. Waymarker posts lead across pasture for some 275yds (251m). Veer right after some woodland, gently up, then down to the left-hand corner stile, Point Ⓑ.

Turn left. Just beyond a private, floodlit tennis court turn right, signposted 'Worc Way South'. Now go straight for 750yds (686m). Turn left at the road. On a bend, where the road is widened for a quarry entrance, do not take the steep flight of wooden steps, but go 80yds (73m) further, downhill, to follow a Worcestershire Way marker, Point Ⓒ. Follow this in woodland for 650yds (594m), then slant across one field before climbing **Abberley Hill**. You may notice that the trees around you – horse chestnuts – are classically coppiced. In one place this ascent is particularly steep, with views to the adjacent deep quarry. Having attained the ridge, keep on it for about ½ mile (800m) until a T-junction of paths, distinguished by a Worcestershire Way sign on a single post and four trees growing in a line across the path just before it. Rejoin Walk 18 here, Point ⑥.

Battle at Powick Bridge

A walk based on one of Worcestershire's most significant historic landmarks.

•DISTANCE•	6½ miles (10.4km)
•MINIMUM TIME•	3hrs
•ASCENT / GRADIENT•	195ft (60m) ▲ ▲ ▲
•LEVEL OF DIFFICULTY•	🏃 🏃🏃 🏃🏃
•PATHS•	Pastures, field paths, minor lanes, 14 stiles
•LANDSCAPE•	Mostly riverside and gentle slopes
•SUGGESTED MAP•	aqua3 OS Explorer 204 Worcester & Droitwich Spa
•START / FINISH•	Grid reference: SO 834522
•DOG FRIENDLINESS•	Mostly sheep pastures, but off lead in middle of walk
•PARKING•	Car park, unsigned, beside A449 roundabout near Powick
•PUBLIC TOILETS•	None on route

Walk 20 Directions

Powick Bridge is an historic place. Mills have stood here since the 11th century or earlier. The big mill-leat, clear on the OS map, was cut in 1291, and great ironworks used the water – but more of that later.

Begin by heading upstream beside the **River Teme**. Barely a mile (1.6km) to the east, it meets the Severn – the site of the Battle of Worcester in 1651, which resolved the Civil War that had blighted the country since 1642. Charles I had been executed in 1649. His heir, Charles II, had returned from exile in France to drum up support, primarily among the Scottish army and die-hard Royalists, to overthrow Cromwell's Parliamentary forces. Die hard they did.

WHILE YOU'RE THERE ⓘ

Bennett's Farm Park is very near, on fields once soaked in battle blood. Apart from the animals, it has a small wooded park, a children's adventure play area and an ice cream 'factory'.

After just 200yds (183m) leave the river to go under the bypass. In the far corner of this meadow move right, beside huge trees perhaps standing in water as the meadow is prone to flooding. Go through a gate and waymarked stile ahead, not to the right, and another set away to the left. Cross two very large meadows. In the third field go to the top corner by walking right, round two edges. A stile gives into the once busy **Lord's Wood**. Hazels were coppiced and oaks were left to stand, many now festooned with ivy. Our route follows a discernible woodlanders' lane.

After 300yds (274m) stiles zig-zag out of Lord's Wood. Soon pass a solitary house, then turn left on the public road (views of Worcester Cathedral). Fork right 30yds (27m) beyond the signs 'Powick' and '30'. A few paces past the **Three Nuns** pub take the unsigned track. At the first bend take a stile, half right. Walk along a left-hand field edge. Passing a house, aim for the far right field corner. Along this right-hand field edge, after 140yds (128m) ignore a low waymarker post; after another 240yds (219m) reach a broad field entrance on the right, but turn left, aiming for a stile half-way down the block of woodland. Out of the trees, go forward 60yds (55m), striking three-quarters right to a footbridge behind a telegraph pole. Skirt right of **Elms** (farm), picking up its driveway to the **A449**.

> ### WHERE TO EAT AND DRINK
> Try the **Three Nuns** at Collett's Green, the **Halfway House** (at the crossing of the A449), the **Red Lion Inn** in Powick village or Powick **village stores**.

Turn right briefly, then cross this fast road carefully, to go perhaps 350yds (320m) along **Ridgeway Farm**'s driveway to a fingerpost. Walk 220yds (201m) up the left-hand field edge, then pass into meadow. Briefly, go close to **Carey's Brook**, later moving to the right-hand field edge. Go over a corner stile, initially slightly uphill, for two fields. A stile beside a rusted gate gives on to a very wide, green lane. Through another gate in 75yds (69m) – not the pylon field – walk along the right-hand field edge. At a pond turn left. After **Broadfields Farm** follow its driveway for 400yds (366m) to a cattle grid. Over this, move immediately down to the right. Walk round the young deciduous plantation, then one arable field to the **B4424**.

Turn right on the pavement for 60yds (55m). Cross to a gate and overgrown stile. Turn left, parallel to the road into **Powick**. After about 300yds (274m) turn down any convenient track, then turn left at the field boundary. Enter St Peter's churchyard by a metal kissing gate. From the outside the stonework of different building

phases is very noticeable, a mixture of 12th-, 15th- and 18th-century building. In Powick itself, the unknown Edward Elgar led the band at the mental asylum, writing compositions for it too.

The route goes straight past the church door, beside more graves, to another kissing gate. Go ahead on a level path (not down to the right); this becomes a service road to the **A449**. You want 'Public footpath, Bransford' up to the left, but cross using traffic-lights to the right. Pass Severn Trent Water's Powick Hams installation, then take a waymarked path through young woodland on the small escarpment for about ¼ mile (400m). Wooden steps lead down to the flood plain. Strike diagonally right, to the underpass and the car park, but you've not quite finished yet!

> ### WHAT TO LOOK FOR
> Inspect the **tower** at Powick's church for battle scars – small craters at about head height and, higher up, marks from small cannon, thought to have been fired by Parliamentarians when Scottish soldiers were using the tower as a look-out.

Stroll along the old and disappearing road to **Powick Bridge** (the 'new' one dates from 1837). Here a plaque, unveiled as recently as 2001, commemorates the men who fought in vain in 1651. A little further, on the left, is the magnificent former hydro-electric power station, first built as a mill, and on the site of generations of mills before it. Now private residences, it is a rare case of a tasteful conversion. In fact, externally, virtually nothing has been changed – balconies have been added, and (not pretty but) essential roof-windows.

Bewdley's Rails and Trails

Take the Severn Valley Railway and walk back through the Wyre Forest.

•DISTANCE•	8½ miles (13.7km)
•MINIMUM TIME•	4hrs
•ASCENT / GRADIENT•	655ft (200m) ▲▲▲
•LEVEL OF DIFFICULTY•	👥 👥 👥
•PATHS•	Forest tracks, field paths, minor lanes, riverside, 8 stiles
•LANDSCAPE•	Undulating woodland, riverside, small town
•SUGGESTED MAP•	aqua3 OS Explorer 218 Wyre Forest & Kidderminster
•START•	Grid reference: SO 764799 (Arley Station)
•FINISH•	Grid reference: SO 791753 (Bewdley Station)
•DOG FRIENDLINESS•	A train ride: yippee! Fun in forest too
•PARKING•	Severn Valley Railway station, Bewdley (patrons only)
•PUBLIC TOILETS•	At station; also Load Street (short-stay) car park in Bewdley

BACKGROUND TO THE WALK

Flooding a market for manufactured goods with imports is not a particularly modern phenomenon – back in the late 19th century, owners of woodland in the Wyre Forest were complaining about cheaper, Continental oak bark eroding their trade. Close to the Industrial Revolution's heartland and a large population, the Wyre Forest had been an important area for the tanning of leather (and for charcoal production, ► Walk 13).

Tanning, the transformation of animal hides or skins into stable, non-porous and durable leather, is a long, multi-staged and labour-intensive process. Dead animals rot quickly – once removed from the slaughtered animal, the flesh has to be cured by salting or drying (or both). At the tannery it is washed and/or adequate moisture is reabsorbed. When oak bark was used skins were left in the tanning vat for anything from typically two days to 90 days. The final 'dressing' stage may involve dyeing, rolling and polishing.

Tannic acid – or tannin – is found in many plants, for example in the fruits of apples and the barks of trees. Tannin levels in trees vary among the species, but oak has the highest concentration, and was therefore the choice among woodlanders supplying tanneries.

By the early 20th century, demand for timber oak had already fallen because of widespread availability of coal for heating and industrial applications, and iron had displaced it as the favoured shipbuilding material, but demand was propped up by the need for oak bark for tanning. Oak bark had to compete with synthetic tanning agents and the use of other, naturally occurring substances such as fish oil (which oxidises on drying, and is the agent used for chamois leather) and mineral-based agents such as chromium sulphate. The introduction of synthetic and cleverly imitative materials reduced the demand for real leather. The tannery in Bewdley was operational until 1928. The centre of Worcester also had a large tannery, called the Three Springs Tannery. In the 21st century, oak bark is almost obsolete as a tanning agent.

In Bewdley the Guildhall houses the tourist information centre and the vibrant Bewdley Museum, focusing on traditional crafts, such as coopering, basket-making and bark peeling. The museum is laid out along a cobbled alleyway. Among its exhibits are old agricultural machinery, a saw-pit and a working hand pump.

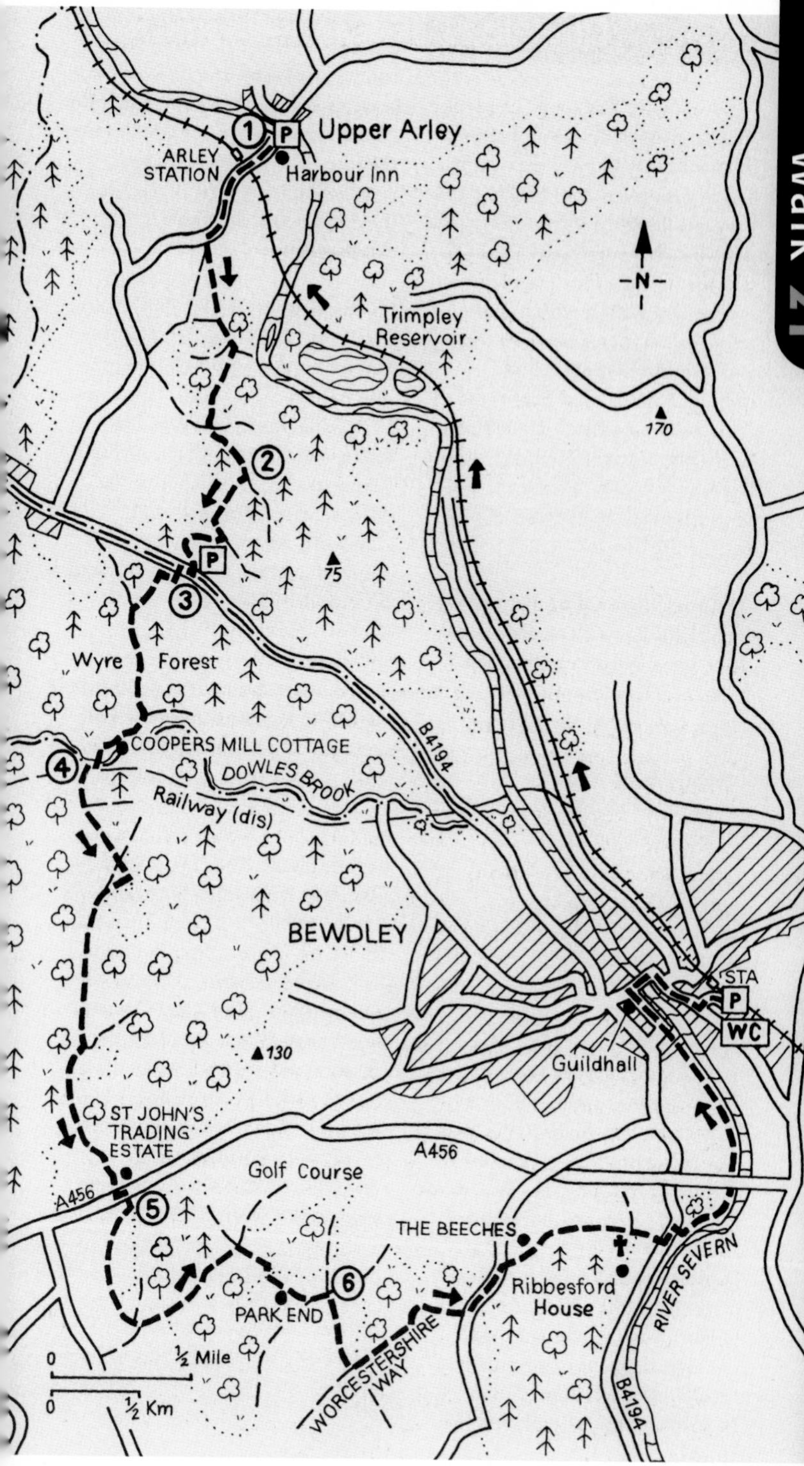

Upper Arley

ARLEY STATION

Harbour Inn

Trimpley Reservoir

▲ 170

–N–

② ▲ 75

③

Wyre   Forest

COOPERS MILL COTTAGE

DOWLES BROOK

Railway (dis)

④

B4194

BEWDLEY

▲ 130

STA

WC

Guildhall

ST JOHN'S TRADING ESTATE

A456

Golf Course

THE BEECHES

Ribbesford House

RIVER SEVERN

⑤

⑥

PARK END

WORCESTERSHIRE WAY

A456

B4194

0   ½ Mile

0   ½ Km

Walk 21

Walk 21 Directions

① From Arley Station go uphill for 700yds (640m). Turn left. Follow a track into woodland. Take a path beside the driveway of **Seckley Cottage**. Roughly 30yds (27m) after right-hand open ground ceases, take the left-hand fork (go left of a broken silver birch with a spot of red paint on it, not between this and a similarly spotted but unbroken tree). Soon bear right. After 440yds (402m) turn left at a track. Just 35yds (32m) on, reach a five-way junction. Go ahead, between posts. In 310yds (280m) reach a fire break.

② About 40yds (37m) beyond this turn right, down a conifer avenue. After some 440yds (402m), at a plantation corner, turn right. At the car park go out to the **B4194**.

> ### WHILE YOU'RE THERE ⓘ
> To visit **The Arboretum** in Upper Arley, part of the legacy of Mr Roger Turner (who died only in 1999), go downhill from Arley's station, across the Severn. **Bewdley** is sufficiently visited to have its own sticks of rock, lettered all the way through, made by Teddy Gray of Dudley.

③ Take a few paces right then cross over. Go only 15yds (14m) into the forest and turn right. Before a house turn left (fingerpost), soon joining a better track. (You are in Shropshire but the trees look much the same.) Keep on this for over ½ mile (800m), descending to **Dowles Brook**'s miniature flood plain. Turn right for under ¼ mile (400m), passing **Coopers Mill Cottage**, then left to a concrete footbridge. Turn immediately right. In 90yds (82m), ascend steeply to an old railway.

④ Go through the gate opposite. After about 650yds (594m) you'll come to a cleared area and new fencing. Your path is half-right, into conifers. Follow this for over ½ mile (800m). Skirt a large clearing. A gravel drive eventually reaches the A456 beside **St John's Trading Estate**.

⑤ Turn left for 75yds (69m) then turn right. Just 30yds (27m) past a 'private garden' sign, take the stile into pasture then another into an abandoned orchard. Instead of taking a third, go perhaps 30yds (27m) further, to another in the corner. Yet another leads into woodland. At a junction turn left ('English Nature' board). Go ahead for 650yds (594m). Near a golf course building turn right. At a yellow-topped pole, marked '39' with a waymarker, turn two-thirds right. Go past the small **Park End** cottage. Turn left, now on tarmac, until you are under power lines.

⑥ Go down a huge field, to a gap in trees about 10yds (9m) wide. Turn left. Follow this for nearly ½ mile (800m) to a road. Turn left. In 350yds (320m) take the right fork, 'Worcestershire Way'. Avoid **The Beeches** using stiles. Descend to Ribbesford's church. A horse chestnut avenue leads to the (fast) **B4194**. Turn left, crossing after 110yds (100m). Follow the **River Severn** into **Bewdley**. Cross Telford's stylish bridge, following signs to the Severn Valley Railway.

> ### WHERE TO EAT AND DRINK ⓘ
> **Arley Station** at the start, or the nearby Harbour Inn. In Bewdley are the Merchant Tearooms, the Cock and Magpie, the Riverside Café, the Mug House, the Merchant's Fish Bar and the Angel pub.

Marvels Around Martley

Contemplate the meaning of cider while striding along a marvellous, airy stretch of Worcestershire's countryside.

•DISTANCE•	6¾ miles (10.9km)
•MINIMUM TIME•	3hrs
•ASCENT / GRADIENT•	720ft (219m) ▲▲▲
•LEVEL OF DIFFICULTY•	🚶 🚶 🚶
•PATHS•	Field paths, lanes, orchard paths, tracks, river meadows, minor roads, 20 stiles
•LANDSCAPE•	Arable, orchards, wooded ridges and Teme Valley
•SUGGESTED MAP•	aqua3 OS Explorer 204 Worcester & Droitwich Spa
•START / FINISH•	Grid reference: SO 766597
•DOG FRIENDLINESS•	Off-lead opportunities if under control
•PARKING•	St Peter's Church, Martley
•PUBLIC TOILETS•	None on route

BACKGROUND TO THE WALK

Don't believe everything you read in your dictionary. In mine the entry for 'cyder' reads 'Same as cider'. The entry for 'wine' is scarcely less controversial: 'The fermented juice of grapes; a liquor made from other fruits.' If you can accept that grapes are not an essential ingredient of wine, then our 'cyder' is apple wine; if you can't, then it's fermented apple juice. Authentic, old-fashioned cyder is virtually extinct. Some of the smaller manufacturers retain the old word, for example, William Gaymer's Bristol Cyder, and Chevallier's Aspall Suffolk Cyder. The latter contains a heady 7 per cent alcohol by volume, but Weston's Special Vintage Cider Reserve is a dizzying 8.2 per cent.

Mrs Beeton
While being no real authority on drink, Mrs Beeton, writing in my grandmother's inter-war edition of Mrs Beeton's Family Cookery, gives a recipe for cider in which there are just two ingredients, cider apples and water, whereas the adjacent page has a recipe for apple wine, which has three ingredients: sugar, water and… cider. In other words, apple wine is 'cider squared' – a twice fermented-out cider. (By the way, the same publication suggests that one of your servants should clean the silver every Friday.) In the cyder-making process some water was added, because firstly a glutinous pulp was unworkable, and secondly even the hard-working enzymes of farm labourers would not maintain sobriety for (say) scything the corn when drinking copious quantities of a heady ferment.

Sickly Water
Cyder was often a safer drink than water, the purity of which might not be assured. The acids in the cyder would have killed off any water-borne diseases. In 1901, when making a critical assessment of the diet offered to inmates of the Dore Workhouse (▶ Walk 41), its medical officer wrote: 'Cold water is a sickly thing to have to drink, especially for agricultural people used to cider.' He may not have meant that there was anything wrong with the water, but his comment shows the ubiquitous nature of cider as a drink at that time.

Goodbye Cyder, Hello Cider

As you walk through one of Bulmers' orchards, it's mind-boggling to think that the Bulmers brothers began with just one acre (0.4ha) in 1888 (▶ Walk 40). In fact, nowadays Herefordshire and Worcestershire's orchards only provide a fraction of the Hereford plant's capacity. The company imports a lot of apple juice concentrate from France, Normandy in particular.

Modern-day 'cider' has sugar added and – what really gets up the nose of the present-day connoisseur – it's almost certainly been fizzed up with carbon dioxide. Even the small print on a can of Bulmers (gassy) Strongbow runs 'dry cider with sugars and sweetener' because the 21st-century palate wouldn't like cyder – they should know.

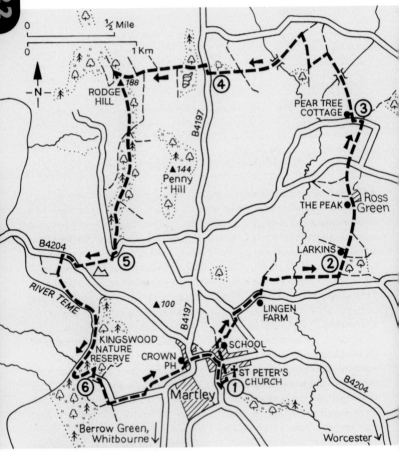

Walk 22 **Directions**

① Go up through the churchyard to the **B4204**. Cross to a rough track. In 100yds (91m) enter the school's grounds briefly, then walk in trees, parallel. Turn right at a stile, then another, to re-enter the grounds. Briefly follow the left edge of the playing fields, then yet another stile gives on to a field. At the road turn left. Turn right, signposted 'Highfields'. Beside **Lingen Farm** go down a track. At the bend take a stile, straight across the field. Cross a stream, then ascend, taking the right-hand gates. Reach a minor road.

② Turn left. At **Larkins** go ahead. At **The Peak** walk behind Ross Green's gardens. Cross fields to reach another road. Go straight over, to a partially concealed stile, not diagonally to a prominent fingerpost. Walk beside a barn, then forward to another lane. Turn left to reach a fingerpost pointing into the apple orchard before the defiantly named **Pear Tree Cottage**.

③ Follow waymarkers carefully through the trees, descending gently. Emerge at a bridge over a ditch, beside apple-sorting equipment. Go 220yds (201m) up this track, to a gap in evergreens. Turn left, down an orchard ride. At a T-junction turn right, up to just before a gate beside a small house. Turn left, almost back on yourself. Go through the orchard, following faded yellow splodges about 1½ft (45cm) up on the tree trunks, but sometimes obscured by low branches. Leave by a footbridge, crossing fields to the **B4197**.

④ Turn right for 60yds (55m). Take an excellent track for ½ mile (800m) to **Rodge Hill**'s top. Turn sharp left, 'Worcs Way South'. Follow this for

1 mile (1.6km). Steps lead down to a road's hairpin bend.

⑤ Turn right. In 20yds (18m) turn left, but in only 15yds (14m) turn right again, into conifers. Emerge to drop down steeply. At the **B4204** turn right for 200yds (183m). Turn left, skirt an enormous barn to the left, then go diagonally to the **River Teme**. Follow this beautiful riverside walk, later in **Kingswood Nature Reserve**, for over ½ mile (800m). Leave the river when a wire fence requires it. Ascend a path, later a driveway, to a tarmac road.

⑥ Turn right, uphill; this soon bends left. Near the brow move right (waymarker) just to walk in the field, not on the road. At the end turn left but, in 275yds (251m), cross two stiles beside a caravan. Beside fields and allotments, emerge between the **Crown** and the garage. Pass the telephone box into the village, then turn right to the church and the start of the walk.

Ravenshill Reserve

Discover a 'mover and shaker' who changed her life and realised a dream.

•DISTANCE•	2¾ miles (4.4km)
•MINIMUM TIME•	1hr 30min
•ASCENT / GRADIENT•	475ft (145m) ▲ ▲ ▲
•LEVEL OF DIFFICULTY•	👣 👣 👣
•PATHS•	Firm or muddy tracks, meadows, some very short but steep, slippery sections, very little road, 8 stiles
•LANDSCAPE•	Woodlands and rolling green fields
•SUGGESTED MAP•	aqua3 OS Explorer 204 Worcester & Droitwich Spa
•START / FINISH•	Grid reference: SO 739539
•DOG FRIENDLINESS•	On leads near livestock, off leads in wooded areas (on leads in Nature Reserve, Walk 24)
•PARKING•	Ravenshill Woodland Reserve (donation)
•PUBLIC TOILETS•	At start

BACKGROUND TO THE WALK

You might think that all you need do to set up a woodland reserve is to acquire some land, buy some trees, and persuade some people to help you plant them. It isn't quite as easy as that, a fact attested by the story of Ravenshill Woodland Reserve. Having opted for early retirement from her high-street-name directorship in 1966, Elizabeth Barling set out to do something innovative and completely different. She did have the advantage of starting out with 94 inherited acres (38ha), negotiating the purchase of a little more to round the acreage up to 100 (40ha). However, conservation is a modern concept – most of the land, once ancient woodland, had been stripped of mature trees in 1929, when national stocks of timber were still recovering from the First World War. In 1966 it was a disorderly mass of spindly, regenerated, mixed native species.

The best part of a year was spent living on a houseboat while taking an MSc in Recreation Management at Loughborough University before implementing her ideas. The greatest setback was the loss of her house in the woods, reduced to a large pile of ashes. Ironically, all this destruction occurred one evening while the owner was in Worcester Cathedral enjoying a performance of Haydn's *Creation*.

Services to Conservation

Look at the suggested map carefully and you will see the word 'Ravenshill' several times, but only once are the birds in the plural, at Ravenshill Wood. In some ways this is an error, but it is not of the Ordnance Survey's making. A bronze name plate had been ordered, and a rogue 's' had appeared on it; this was pointed out to Miss Barling but she decided to keep the distinction. Later, Ordnance Survey fieldworkers re-mapping the area were shown that 'Ravenshill' was indeed the correct spelling. The information building is rustic and a little ramshackle, but has wall-to-wall wildlife displays, and empathetically invites you to borrow wellington boots (various sizes available) free of charge. Establishing Ravenshill Woodland Reserve was certainly a labour of love. The full story is set down in her book, *Birth of a Nature Reserve*, published in 1982. She was recognised with an MBE in 1978 for her services to conservation. Happily, the present owners and the Worcestershire Wildlife Trust have carried forward her philosophy into the reserve's present-day management. Elizabeth Barling's legacy is there, waiting for you to enjoy it.

The reserve is open daily from April to October and at weekends only from November to March. The distance given in the information panel does not include walking the 1/2 mile (800m) red trail or 1 1/2 mile (2.4km) blue trail in the reserve itself.

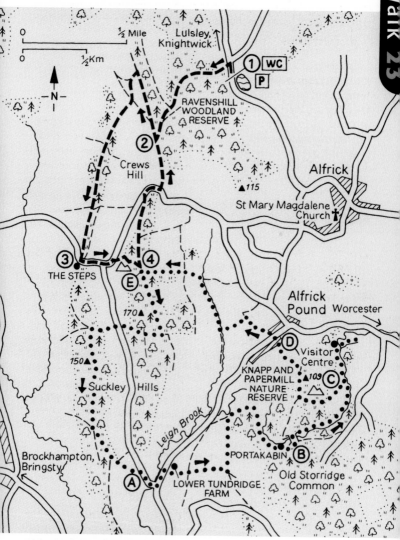

Walk 23 Directions

① Walk towards Lulsley for roughly 150yds (137m). Turn left on a green track beside **Hill Orchard**'s private

drive. Soon in woods, go 500yds (457m) or so, joining another track beside some wire enclosures. When a stile and nearby gate lead into a field on the right, go just 20yds (18m) further. Now go up to the

Walk 23

left on a path (you may spot a yellow band on a branch). In 120yds (110m) climb a rustic stile to turn partially right. Note well this point, where a path joins obliquely from the left, since you'll be returning this way – the junction is easily missed! Go on for 100yds (91m) to a driveway. Walk for 30yds (27m) away from the house, to follow the sign, 'bridleway', down to the right. Soon, at a line of incongruous laurel bushes, reach the tree-lined Worcestershire Way.

> **WHERE TO EAT AND DRINK** ⓘ
> Just ½ mile (800m) north of the start is the **Fox and Hounds** in Lulsley, with an enclosed beer garden. Alfrick's **post office and stores**, in a prime location at the village crossroads, is a vibrant place, generously supplied with fruit. At Knightwick is the **Talbot**.

② Turn right. After 650yds (594m) go through a gate. Peel left, hugging the trees but not going under them. A narrow gap would lead into a second meadow but on the right is a fenced area, guarded by a sinewy field maple. Climb the waymarked stile beside the padlocked gate. After another gate ascend diagonally right, veering left as it levels. Maintain this line through metal gates across fields, then a wooden gate into woodland. Eventually **The Steps** comes into view. Reach the road by descending beside a paddock fence, then through more gates, including a red one.

③ Turn left. Beyond Threshers Barn and Wain House is **Crews Court**. Here, beside a fingerpost, ascend some wooden steps to a stile that welcomes you with 'Beware butting sheep'. Go ahead, crossing this private garden, to a paddock. Go ahead but slightly right, to a

> **WHAT TO LOOK FOR** ⓘ
> The **reservoir** opposite Ravenshill Woodland Reserve was dug in 1977. Along Leigh Brook the Worcestershire Wildlife Trust has built suitable **holts** (otter houses). You'll need patience (and perhaps a sleeping bag) to catch sight of an otter. On Walk 24, **Lower Tundridge Farm** is a timber-framed building with mullioned and transomed windows. Built in the early 17th century, it was one of the last of its kind, before brick structures became the norm.

padlocked seven-bar metal gate; climb over this. Now move 20yds (18m) right to find your path up – here is the proper stile, rendered obsolete by the new fence across its line to the garden gate. Go up quite steeply – perhaps using hands for the last bit up the earthbank, otherwise find a less steep part. Now at the ridge, don't fall off the unexpectedly wobbly stile here.

④ Turn left. After about 275yds (251m) fork down to the left, not invitingly ahead. At the road cross it before turning right to walk round the bend. Turn left along the driveway of **The Crest**, then move left for the Worcestershire Way again. Follow this to Point ②, then retrace your steps.

> **WHILE YOU'RE THERE** ⓘ
> Alfrick's **Church of St Mary Magdalene** is not of extreme architectural interest, it's merely extremely pretty – mixed stone facing, a wooden bell tower, and original sandstone window casings. Inside are exposed roof beams and much stained-glass of Dutch origin. The **Brockhampton Estate** draws crowds to its 14th-century, moated manor house and timber-framed gatehouse. Gardeners will appreciate the modest 2½ acres (1ha) of largely formal grounds at **The Garden at The Bannut** at Bringsty.

On to the Suckley Hills

This loop takes in a second nature reserve and more of the Worcestershire Way.
See map and information panel for Walk 23

•**DISTANCE**•	4¾ miles (7.7km)
•**MINIMUM TIME**•	2hrs 30min
•**ASCENT / GRADIENT**•	625ft (190m) ▲▲▲
•**LEVEL OF DIFFICULTY**•	🚶🚶🚶

Walk 24 Directions (Walk 23 option)

From Point ④ on Walk 23 continue on the ridge for 550yds (503m), noting Point Ⓔ after 90yds (82m). Turn right to a road. Take the track opposite. Bear right at a junction and, 40yds (37m) beyond, look for an ascending track on the left. Follow this for almost ½ mile (800m). Fork left and down. After walking about 250yds (229m) a gate leads through a meadow to a road, Point Ⓐ.

Turn right and, at a T-junction, turn left. Turn right (no sign) beside **Lower Tundridge Farm**. After 500yds (457m) find a yellow waymarked gatepost. Turn left, along the field edge. Follow these waymarkers, but be sure to turn left at a rutted part of a muddy track in the woods. After a **Portakabin** reach a house's driveway. Turn left but, within a few paces, move right to find a footbridge, Point Ⓑ, among the shrubs. Turn left. At the top turn right. In just 40yds (37m) take a gate back down. Walk beside the brook until a gate at the far end of a meadow, Point Ⓒ. On the right here, through another gate, is a wide, low, grassy footbridge. To see

more of the **Knapp and Papermill Nature Reserve** and its visitor centre walk on (not over the footbridge) another 500yds (457m), then retrace your steps.

Go a quarter right. In the meadow corner a narrow opening leads into woods. In 20yds (18m) fork left, soon rising steeply. It emerges after 180yds (165m) at a large, wooden kissing gate, but don't go through it. Turn right. At a T-junction in 80yds (73m) turn left. Within 50yds (46m), at a skew crossing with a lectern-style notice board, go straight on. Join a path from a substantial hut. Soon a good track leads to **Alfrick Pound**, Point Ⓓ.

Take a fingerpost 20yds (18m) to the left. In the second field turn left, between two large oaks, descending to a footbridge. Turn right. Cross two stiles then a third across a dirt track. Importantly, turn left immediately – don't go beyond a massively girthed willow in front of you. Walk beside the fence for just 20yds (18m). Aim for the right edge of an orchard block, rising gently, taking a stile into the wood behind it. Beware hazardous, old fence wire hereabouts. Go up, veering slightly left through boggy, reedy grass to a T-junction, Point Ⓔ. Turn right, rejoining Walk 23 in 90yds (82m).

Walk 25

Under and Over the Malverns

Take a train to visit Great Malvern, then return over its attractive backdrop.

•DISTANCE•	4½ miles (7.2km)
•MINIMUM TIME•	2hrs 30min
•ASCENT / GRADIENT•	950ft (290m) ▲▲▲
•LEVEL OF DIFFICULTY•	脩 脩 脩
•PATHS•	Streets, railway bed, woodland paths, meadows, 3 stiles
•LANDSCAPE•	Suburban, recreational, wooded and pastoral
•SUGGESTED MAP•	aqua3 OS Explorer 190 Malvern Hills & Bredon Hill
•START•	Grid reference: SO 782457 (Great Malvern Station)
•FINISH•	Grid reference: SO 756424 (Colwall Station)
•DOG FRIENDLINESS•	Few off-lead opportunities, must be controlled on ridge
•PARKING•	Car parks at both railway stations
•PUBLIC TOILETS•	None on route

Walk 25 Directions

Out of Great Malvern Station, go ahead and left in 30yds (27m) into **Imperial Road** (no sign this end).

The presence of spa waters in Malvern had been known for centuries. The seeds of growth were sown in 1756 when a Dr Wall wrote of the waters' benefits. The 1820s saw the opening of the Baths and Pump Room, then the railway in the 1850s brought it to a much wider market. The local architect Edward Wallace Elmslie designed Great Malvern's railway station (1861), considered elegant by the Victorians. Even today the wrought-ironwork of the railway station's mock pillars (actually drainpipes) are maintained in gaudy colours.

Cross **Tiverton Road**, turning right on **Clarence Road**. At the skew junction take **Albert Road South**. At the end turn left. Beside the railway bridge take a leafy alleyway right, beside Malvern College's grounds. Cross the next road, on to **Malvern Common**. In 600yds (549m) pass under the railway. Within a mile (1.6km) from here, the railway enters Colwall Tunnel.

It isn't without reason that the Malvern Hills stand above the Worcestershire Plain. At their centre is a hard rock called pre-Cambrian sienite, flanked by softer red marl and limestone. The people who understood this best were the labourers employed by the Worcester and Hereford Railway to dig the Colwall Tunnel. Work started in 1856 at both ends, meeting in 1860. While an advance of 5ft (1.5m) per day could be made through the outer rocks, the ancient

> ***WHAT TO LOOK FOR***
> The period 1860–2 was very busy for architect **Edward Wallace Elmslie**. Besides Great Malvern's railway station he designed the Malvern Link Hotel (at Malvern Link station) and the Imperial Hotel. The Imperial was purchased by Malvern Girls' College in 1919; Malvern Link became a school in the 1870s.

rock could slow progress to just a tenth of this. Over its total length of 1,567yds (1,432m) it climbed 58ft (18m). The chief engineer on the project was Stephen Ballard, who, in the previous two decades, had overseen the Hereford and Gloucester Canal (▶ Walk 27).

As the railway line veers right, keep ahead to a road. Turn left for 30yds (27m). Follow a fingerpost closely, through trees to a **cinder path**. After 500yds (457m) descend wooden steps to cross several golf fairways on a slightly raised, green track. In dense woodland turn left – this track leads to the clubhouse and car park. Go diagonally, to the far side of a white building (waymarker). Cross beside a green carefully – beware golf balls zinging from the right – then another fairway, to reach open fields. A pitted concrete track leads to the **A449**. Cross this, and the upper road, to a centre-railed path. At the Y-junction turn left. Here you are almost over the Colwall Tunnel, or rather, tunnels.

> ### WHERE TO EAT AND DRINK ⓘ
> There are several options in Great Malvern. On the route, strategically sited near the popular Gardiners Quarry Car Park is **The Kettle Sings** tea room, and in Colwall itself is the **Crown Inn**.

The brick-lined tunnel was so heavily used by steam locomotives that carriages would emerge with fallen lining bricks on their roofs. This is not the tunnel you ride through today – modern trains take you in a parallel, broader tunnel, built close enough to the original one to use its ventilation shafts by boring linking shafts. Stephen Ballard was buried in his garden at The Winnings in Colwall, above the

western entrance to the tunnel. During the Second World War the old tunnel was used to store ammunition. The new tunnel's spoil was redeployed in 1959 to provide hard core for the M50 motorway which runs from Strensham to Ross-on-Wye.

The road becomes a tarmac track, but fork right on to a path before the house ahead. There are many ways on to the Malverns' ridge – this is just one. Follow the path for 275yds (251m) gently uphill and a further 440yds (402m) on the level. At an X-shape crossing, beside a bright green seat, take the upward right fork that zig-zags. Soon, at a second green seat, continue straight ahead, gently up. After 250yds (229m) of rising gently, take a right and zig-zag gently up to another seat. In 175yds (160m) keep straight ahead and up, ignoring a zig-zagging option up left. Dense woodland gives way to bracken and scattered silver birch. After 180yds (165m) ignore a downward right fork. Back into (less dense) woodland, after 140yds (128m) take an acute left turn, finally to meet the ridge path beside some unexpected pines.

Turn left, soon leaving the gravel path to attain the visible top. Less than 200yds (183m) beyond it, when a path forks right, turn fully right, down a steep ride, zig-zagging to the **B4232** at **Gardiners Quarry car park**.

Take the other tarmac road to **The Kettle Sings** tea room. Turn left in front of it (fingerpost). In 110yds (100m) reach a multiple marker post. Turn right, descending, following the Worcestershire Way for a short ½ mile (800m) to a clear fingerpost signed 'Colwall Station'.

Walk 26

A Long Amble from Mamble

Discover why the Leominster Canal failed to make money for its owners.

•DISTANCE•	10½ miles (16.8km)
•MINIMUM TIME•	5hrs
•ASCENT / GRADIENT•	690ft (210m) ▲ ▲ ▲
•LEVEL OF DIFFICULTY•	🚶 🚶 🚶
•PATHS•	Minor roads, field and woodland paths, tow path, 18 stiles
•LANDSCAPE•	Undulating pastoral landscape
•SUGGESTED MAP•	aqua3 OS Explorer 203 Ludlow
•START / FINISH•	Grid reference: SO 685712
•DOG FRIENDLINESS•	Lead often desirable, and don't forget dog's lunch
•PARKING•	Lay-by (bend in old road) west of Mamble on A456
•PUBLIC TOILETS•	None on route

BACKGROUND TO THE WALK

Crude forms of coal mining were probably first carried out on the land around the small village of Mamble in prehistoric times. Much later, the Blount family lived at Sodington Hall, and the Mamble coal pits were part of their estate.

It may have been the case that mining was a part-time activity for what were primarily farmworkers. The inference drawn from the absence of much housing in the Marl Brook area is that mining was never more than a small-scale activity. Mamble's coal was not of premium quality, but it was adequate for domestic use and non-critical industrial processes such as lime burning. Coal mining continued in the locality until 1972. The last pit to close was the Mole Colliery at Hunthouse, about 1 mile (1.6km) south east of Mamble. The more modern, deep-mining techniques are the ones that cause least disruption at the surface. It is believed that, having won the coal from a pit, the ancient miners put it into wagons, to be hauled by horse along a rudimentary tramway to the (partially constructed) canal.

The rationale for the Leominster Canal, sanctioned by a 1791 Act of Parliament, was simple enough – provide a terminus for the distribution of coal emerging from the pits around Mamble, and reduce the price of conveying other goods between Leominster (pronounced 'Lemsta') and the River Severn. An advertisement displayed in 1797 proclaimed a cost saving, priced per ton, on this route of 25 per cent, and a 'more speedy conveyance'. Indeed, in 1796 the price of coal at Leominster was halved.

Collapsed Plans

On the walk you pass Wharf House, where coal was loaded on to barges. For various reasons, the canal company failed to build nearly all of the remaining eastward section; in particular, the unfinished Southnett Tunnel collapsed. Its position is near Broombank Farm, roughly below Ash Coppice. All manner of constructional defects in this, and in the Rea Aqueduct (Point ⑤), were reported by a consulting engineer. The Rea Aqueduct is still standing; presumably it has been inspected recently, but it's a pretty scary sight!

Not having the Southnett Tunnel cut off access to essential water from Dumbleton Brook (beyond the tunnel's eastern portal) so the Stocking Pool (Point ⑥), a reservoir, was built. The canal was eventually bought by the railway in the late 1850s and wound down.

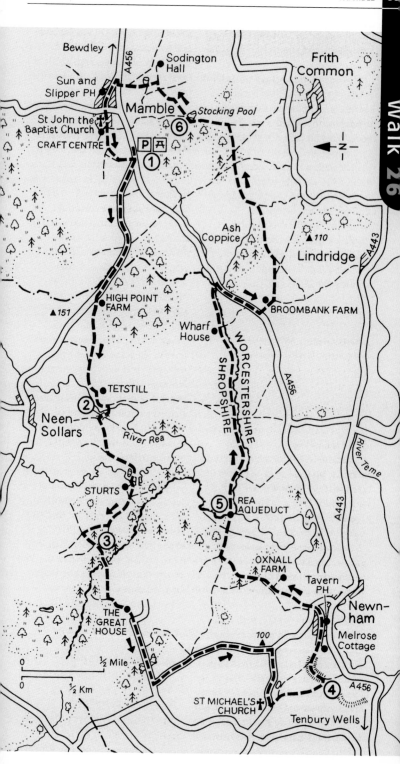

Bewdley ↑

Sun and Slipper PH

St John the Baptist Church

CRAFT CENTRE

Sodington Hall

Mamble

Stocking Pool

⑥

Ⓟ ⛺ ①

Frith Common

←N→

Ash Coppice

▲110

Lindridge

HIGH POINT FARM

▲151

Wharf House

Broombank Farm

WORCESTERSHIRE

SHROPSHIRE

TETSTILL

②

Neen Sollars

River Rea

STURTS

③

⑤ REA AQUEDUCT

THE GREAT HOUSE

OXNALL FARM

Tavern PH

Newnham

Melrose Cottage

100

½ Mile

0

0   ½ Km

ST MICHAEL'S CHURCH

Tenbury Wells ↓

A456

A443

River Teme

④ A456

Walk 26

Walk 26 Directions

① Towards Tenbury, take the minor road. Down **High Point Farm**'s driveway a gate marks an indistinct green lane to **Tetstill**. Turn right. Soon cross an old railway bridge.

② Through two fields, reach a stile. Follow the left field edge. Turn left. Just before Sturts' private bridge go down and right – concrete flagstones lead to a footbridge. Ascend a track left of **Sturts**. At the brow move right, taking the left of two gates. Go to the right edge of conifers. In 220yds (201m), at the next corner, turn left. Aim left of a massive oak, to a gate into conifers.

> **WHERE TO EAT AND DRINK**
> Newnham's **Tavern** has hot and cold food, a beer patio and childrens' play area. Mamble's **Sun and Slipper** has a beer terrace. **Mamble Craft Centre Tea Room** has a lawn with gorgeous views.

③ Descend to cross a wooden footbridge. Keep forward – not over another bridge – soon to return to pasture. In 325yds (297m) turn left. Find a stile through **The Great House**'s gardens. Follow minor roads to **St Michael's Church**. Take the waymarked route, following pylons closely. In 600yds (549m), when descending, cross one stile but turn left at a second (not over it).

④ Follow this old tow path for 275yds (251m). By some exposed earth cross the canal bed (boggy in winter, overgrown in summer). Find a wicket gate to the right. Reach a track, **Tavern Lane**. Where the driveway to **Oxnall Farm** bends, go straight. Of two gates take the lower, right-hand one. In 60yds (55m) keep left. Leave a plantation

at a stile then, importantly, take a gate immediately right. Strike diagonally to an opening. In 10yds (9m) turn right along a track briefly, then go forward to a corner stile into trees. Cross the old railway. The ditch on your left marks the canal. Its brick lining is evident at the next stile. You are now standing on the **Rea Aqueduct**.

⑤ Follow the canal for 1¼ miles (2km). At the A456 turn right. Cross to the old canal bend, taking the public footpath. Leave the driveway at **Broombank Farm**'s gate. Walk along the left edge of several fields, initially in a cherry orchard. At a corner strike half-right to a pylon. Around a dry valley head, keep on the brow, beside a new hedgerow. Move left, to trees shielding a small pond (possibly dry). Ease away from new fencing (now on your right) to a two-bar stile through a plantation strip. Go to the woodland corner. Veer right for 75yds (69m); over this stile, go down to cross the **Stocking Pool**'s dam.

⑥ Go up to the gate in the new fence's left corner. Walk 80yds (73m) to the second (not first) stile. Go forward to the road, turning left then right then left, into **Mamble**. Turn right, then left. Before the craft centre take a fingerpost, squeezing beside Tudor Cottage's garage. After a two-plank brook bridge go up and left, across fields to the Neen Sollars road junction and the lay-by.

> **WHILE YOU'RE THERE**
> The **Mamble Craft Centre** has a stunning array of wares of varying degrees of utility, and four craft workshops attached to it. (My advice is that, if any of your companions are 'shoppers', do the walk first.)

Hereford's Lost Canal

This walk includes a stretch by an abandoned waterway, now being restored.

•DISTANCE•	7¾ miles (12.5km)
•MINIMUM TIME•	3hrs 30min
•ASCENT / GRADIENT•	260ft (79m) ▲ ▲ ▲
•LEVEL OF DIFFICULTY•	🚶 🚶 🚶
•PATHS•	Field and woodland paths, minor roads, at least 35 stiles
•LANDSCAPE•	Gently undulating, mixed farming, woodland, derelict canal
•SUGGESTED MAP•	aqua3 OS Explorer 202 Leominster & Bromyard
•START / FINISH•	Grid reference: SO 642415
•DOG FRIENDLINESS•	Close control near livestock and on minor roads
•PARKING•	St Bartholomew's Church, Ashperton
•PUBLIC TOILETS•	None on route

BACKGROUND TO THE WALK

Unless you know where to look, the only hint of the Hereford and Gloucester Canal in the city of Hereford today is in the street named Canal Road, which led to the canal's western terminus. In the east the canal joined the River Severn at Over, just west of Gloucester. The canal's success was short-lived.

Hereford and Gloucester Canal Trust

Since the 1980s the Hereford and Gloucester Canal Trust has striven to restore the canal to its former glory. The Trust's greatest tangible achievements to date have been restoring the skew bridge at Monkhide, a section of canal at Yarkhill, and the Over Basin, across the border in Gloucestershire. Perhaps the greatest intangible achievement to date has been the partial winning over of opinion. Gradually people in authority are realising that this isn't just men playing with water and boats instead of railways and steam trains (and not just because some of the canal volunteers are women). Perhaps it's because they have noticed the thriving and growing canal leisure sector in adjacent Worcestershire (► Walks 3 and 17), where almost as many people overnight on boats (13 per cent) as they do in bed and breakfast accommodation (14 per cent). A few years ago the planning authorities were successfully lobbied in Hereford city. The service road to a new retail park in the north of the city – connecting Newtown Road and Burcott Road – includes a bridge that spans the course of the old canal, instead of cutting through it or filling it with hardcore or concrete. Most recently, Herefordshire Council's blueprint for redeveloping the northern part of Hereford's city centre proposes restoration of the canal basin.

Ballard's Skew Bridge

Inspired by photographs, I went to see the skew bridge at Monkhide. Do this yourself and, like me, you'll surely be disappointed. True, it's on private land, but no provision has been made for access – in short, you can't legitimately take a good look at engineer Stephen Ballard's mini-masterpiece, now a Grade II listed building. Ballard later worked as a railway engineer (► Walk 25). His grandson, also called Stephen, unveiled a plaque on the bridge. It's a shame that the skew bridge hasn't been made into a modest 'place to visit'.

Not a Bad Deal

Records show that, typically, a lock keeper would be paid 14s per week but his employers would deduct 2s per week for rent. Lock cottages may have been rudimentary, but what could someone today earning, say, £350 per week rent for £50 per week? This brings to mind the old but still valid expression, 'the best place to put your money is in bricks and mortar' – house bricks, that is, not canal bricks.

Walk 27 **Directions**

① From the church car park take the 'forty shillings' gate, behind houses. (For all of ten paces the path is actually in a garden.) Join a track to the **A417**. Turn left, then right, beside a driveway. Follow a fingerpost across meadows for about 600yds (549m). Find a gate beside a cricket net. Veer right.

Cross a driveway down a long field. Join **Haywood Lane** near a house. Turn left. Follow this for roughly 1 mile (1.6km). Find a stile on the left just beyond a gate about 100yds (91m) after the driveway leading to **Upleadon Court**.

② Cross large arable fields and a ditch, then **Upleadon Farm**'s driveway. Aim for the far left-hand corner, then skirt some woodland to your left, later striking left (waymarked) up a huge field. At **Gold Hill Farm** go right of a tall shed. Behind this, turn left then briefly up and right. Follow a boundary remnant to a road.

> ### WHERE TO EAT AND DRINK ⓘ
> About ½ mile (800m) south of Ashperton is the **Hopton Arms Inn**. It serves bar meals and also has a restaurant. You can also get tea and coffee here. There is a beer terrace (beside the main road) and a separate children's play area.

③ Turn left for ¼ mile (400m). Where the road turns left go ahead for a short ½ mile (800m), initially beside a wood. Over a rotting plank turn left but in 25yds (23m) turn right. After 500yds (457m) enter trees. On leaving them strike half right for **White House**.

④ Turn right along the road. When you reach the junction, take the footpath opposite (there's a ditch on your right). Beware (please!) of the chance to smash your head on a

> ### WHAT TO LOOK FOR ⓘ
> Near the cricket net and the road beyond it are the **Ashperton Tunnel** portals, in a deep cutting, dug in 1840 – presumably the unnatural heaps thereabouts are canal spoil. You should see some **solar panels** in use near Gold Hill Farm.

horizontal tree trunk just after concentrating on a single-plank footbridge. Walk another 700yds (640m) across fields, over three footbridges and under power lines, passing through a gap to another stile, but do not cross this – note three waymarkers on its far side. Turn left, heading towards old orchards. Just beyond **Homend** find a stile in a far left-hand corner, shielded by a huge ash and a persistent elder. Turn left, soon moving right to double gates flanking a wide concrete bridge. After the leafy avenue keep ahead, eventually veering right. Go 550yds (503m), crossing the driveway to **Canon Frome Court**, then another track, finally reaching a road by a spinney.

⑤ Cross over the road and walk straight to the canal. Turn left. In 140yds (128m) turn right, over the canal. Veer left and uphill, finding a large oak in the top left-hand corner. Keep this line despite the field boundary shortly curving away. On reaching a copse turn right, later moving left into an indistinct lane. The village hall heralds the **A417**. Turn left, along the pavement. Turn right to the church and the car park at the start of the walk.

> ### WHILE YOU'RE THERE ⓘ
> The **Hop Pocket Craft Centre** at Bishop's Frome (also near Walks 28 and 29) is a mecca for craftspeople and artists, providing workshops, studios and shop windows for handcrafted wares. The centre, in converted farm buildings, has expanded, largely due to a six-figure Rural Enterprise grant awarded in 2002, to cover some 40 per cent of the conversion costs. You'll also find locally made food and drink here such as cheeses, game, wines and ciders.

Walk 28

Two Frome Valley Churches

Secluded churches with unique features, and special trees amid pastures.

•DISTANCE•	4¾ miles (7.7km)
•MINIMUM TIME•	2hrs 30min
•ASCENT / GRADIENT•	475ft (145m) ▲▲ ▲ ▲
•LEVEL OF DIFFICULTY•	🚶 🚶 🚶
•PATHS•	Field paths, dirt tracks, lanes and minor roads, 14 stiles
•LANDSCAPE•	Orchards, woodlands and pasture in gently rolling hills
•SUGGESTED MAP•	aqua3 OS Explorer 202 Leominster & Bromyard
•START / FINISH•	Grid reference: SO 679502
•DOG FRIENDLINESS•	Good early on, but otherwise often among livestock
•PARKING•	Roadside just before grassy lane to Acton Beauchamp's church – please tuck in tightly
•PUBLIC TOILETS•	None on route

BACKGROUND TO THE WALK

At first sight the Church of St Giles at Acton Beauchamp is unremarkable, sitting comfortably on a hillside. Parts of it are Norman, but it was largely rebuilt in 1819. However, if you move to the left of the main door you will see a doorway that leads into the tower. The lintel to this doorway is nothing less than a re-used 9th-century stone sculpture, depicting a bird, a lion, and probably a goat – there is nothing like this from the Anglo-Saxon period in Herefordshire.

Wild Service Trees

Through the gate into the churchyard in Acton Beauchamp, a grassy path slants up to the church. Your eye may follow the shiny black line of the handrail that assists people to and from the church door, but right in front of you is an excellent specimen of a wild service tree. It must have been planted there. Wild service trees actually in the wild are relatively rare nowadays, although it is quite fashionable to plant them in urban settings. Their leaves are easily confused with those of a plane tree, but the latter's bark is very distinctive.

It is rare for the seeds of the wild service tree to have the opportunity to germinate since they are eaten and, genetically, destroyed by wasps. (This is in contrast to the consumption of hawthorn berries by birds, for example, where the expulsion of the seed, intact, after digestion of its juicy berry coating, is an effective form of dispersal.)

Academics are uncertain as to the significance of the name 'service'. Most likely it is a contorted Anglicisation of its Latin name *Sorbus torminalis*. Before multiple varieties of apples became available, wild service trees were grown in orchards because their fruits are edible. My dictionary says that a 'sorb' is a wild service tree, and that its fruits are called 'sorb-apples'. (In the southern counties of England they were called chequers.) Other less convincing theories are that 'service' derives from the Latin 'cervisia' for beer – not far from the contemporary Spanish 'cerveza' – since the wild service fruits were fermented to make a beery drink, really as a predecessor to cyder. Alternatively, it could have some association with the French word for cherry, 'cerise', since, although a kiwi-fruit brown, not red, wild service fruits are of a size and shape comparable to cherries.

In Stanford Bishop, St James' Church is similarly isolated, but has a hilltop position. The stonework is of a similar vintage to that in Acton Beauchamp – Norman and 13th century. Several yew trees dominate the churchyard, the mightiest of which is said to be 1,200 years old; inside, you'll see a certificate to this effect. Also here, nestling in a corner, is the strikingly well preserved, capacious wooden chair said to be used by St Augustine in the year AD 603.

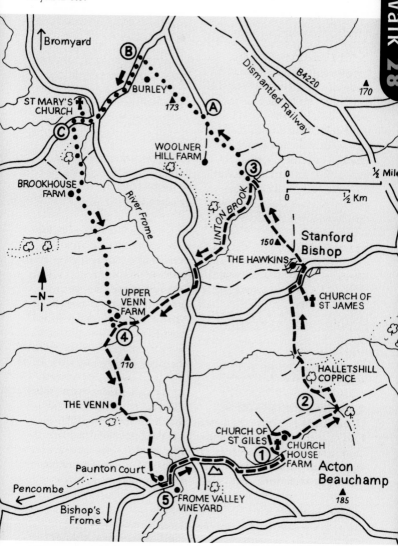

Walk 28 Directions

① Leave the churchyard by an iron gate in the top corner. Soon enter an orchard. Skirt round to the right,

passing outbuildings of **Church House Farm** and then down to pass behind tall barns. Now the orchard track ascends. When 110yds (100m) beyond power lines, at the corner of a plantation, turn left (blue waymarker), to walk between orchard rows. At the end turn left. In roughly 160yds (146m), well before the power lines and just before trees shielding a pond, go right. Soon you'll have a hedge on your left; reach a gate and a stile of three railway sleepers.

② Once through **Halletshill Coppice** drop straight down to a footbridge. Now go straight up the bank, swapping hedge sides, to a minor road. Turn right (and visit the church). Return to the road and turn right. At the entrance to **The Hawkins** take a stile, then follow waymarkers across a track to skirt this farm. Now head down the pastures to cross a footbridge over the **Linton Brook**. (Walk 29 leaves at this point.)

WHAT TO LOOK FOR ⓘ

Apart from orchards you'll also see **hop fields** on this walk and, in the vicinity of Paunton Court, look through the hedgerows for **vineyards**. They belong to Frome Valley Vineyard. Established only in 1992, the product of a modest 4 acres (1.6ha) goes into the making of four dry wines, one medium sweet and a rosé.

---

③ Turn left, walking beside the **Linton Brook** for ⅝ mile (1km), to a road. Turn left for 160yds (146m). Turn right. Now the driveway to **Upper Venn Farm** runs for ½ mile (800m). Just before the farm

---

WHERE TO EAT AND DRINK ⓘ

Such is the effort required to find the diminutive **Majors' Arms** at Halmonds Frome that you might hope that drinks would be on the house. It's worth paying for the views alone. On the B4214 through Bishop's Frome, the **Chase Inn** has Bulmers' Original, Wye Valley's beer and Frome Valley Vineyard's wine. Dogs allowed in the beer garden. Behind it, hidden from the B road, the family-run **Green Dragon** sells Theakston's and Foster's. Hot drinks and jacket potatoes at **Shortwood Family Farm** are very reasonably priced.

---

buildings move left, to a stile roughly 70yds (64m) along the edge of the field from the farm. (Walk 29 rejoins here.)

④ Cross the field diagonally, to a gate in the left hedge. Turn left across a field, aiming slightly uphill, beside residual mature oaks. You'll find a stile beyond an electricity pole. Pick up a rough track to **The Venn**. Admire its cream walls and exposed timbers, then turn away, along the drive. Follow this down to the minor road.

⑤ Turn left, passing **Frome Valley Vineyard** on a sharp bend. At the crossroads go straight over. Climbing this quite steep lane, the **Church of St Giles** comes into view. Take the first turning on the left to return to your car.

WHILE YOU'RE THERE ⓘ

Over 300 rose varieties are at nearby **Acton Beauchamp Roses**. To the west, south of Pencombe, is the fabulous **Shortwood Family Farm**. Younger children will happily consume a whole day at this complete hands-on livestock experience and in its play barn. Everything the farm produces is organic and you can join in collecting eggs, feeding the young animals and milking cows and goats. In late October horses work the cider mill. **Bromyard**, a 'black-and-white' market town for centuries, has recently acquired a veneer of eccentricity with the launch of a Public Art Trail – it's certainly contemporary, in that it combines the appropriate with the frankly silly. Lastly, don't forget Bishop's Frome's **Hop Pocket Craft Centre** (► Walk 27).

A Frome Valley Church Ruin

Linger longer in the Frome Valley and visit a creepy ruin.
See map and information panel for Walk 28

•DISTANCE•	6¼ miles (10.1km)
•MINIMUM TIME•	3hrs 15min
•ASCENT / GRADIENT•	655ft (200m) ▲▲ ▲ ▲
•LEVEL OF DIFFICULTY•	🚶🚶 🚶🚶 🚶

Walk 29 Directions (Walk 28 option)

At Point ③ cross the stile then turn left up the field edge. Where two stiles span the hedge turn left (waymarked), resuming along the field edge. At a cluster of gates below a power line go on to the tarmac, Point Ⓐ.

To your left is a cattle grid and driveway to **Woolner Hill Farm**. Beside it are two gates – take the right-hand one. Use this grassy track for just 25yds (23m), then take the stile on the right here. Waymarkers are initially clear, but in a field with a telegraph pole towards the left corner, veer right to walk down the right side of a line of trees (hidden single waymarker on a tall post). Now bear left through these trees – pass the building, **Burley**, about 110yds (100m) to your left. Continue to reach a minor road, Point Ⓑ.

Turn left. Go steadily down this gated road. About 150yds (137m) beyond the crossroads is the decayed avenue leading to the even more decayed church. **St Mary's Church** appears as a shamefully abandoned ruin. In fact, the church is a Scheduled Ancient Monument and a Category A, Grade II listed building, but it's the usual story of not enough money to go round. To add insult to injury, at the entrance of the avenue was an unsightly pile of dead car components (in autumn 2002). A path leads into an area of graves and tombstones, worthy of a Hammer horror set – you expect one of the tombs to pop open at any moment. Of the church itself, only parts of three contiguous walls and a couple of Norman windows remain.

Back on the lane, go 80yds (73m) further to a stile on the left, Point Ⓒ. Skirt round the plantation of primarily ash trees. Join the driveway to **Brookhouse Farm**, then yellow triangles guide you through it. Walk beside a very young orchard. Look for a wooden handrail and footbridge within 200yds (183m), switching the field boundary to your right. After 400yds (366m), where an option is to go left, keep straight on. Now keep pretty straight for a good ¼ mile (400m). Pass to the right of the buildings of **Upper Venn Farm**. Do not start down the driveway but walk along the right edge of the field which it crosses for roughly 70yds (64m) to a stile. Here you rejoin Walk 28.

Walk 30

Woolhope and Sollers Hope

A down-and-round-and-up walk in a peaceful farming area.

•DISTANCE•	6 miles (9.7km)
•MINIMUM TIME•	2hrs 45min
•ASCENT / GRADIENT•	525ft (160m) ▲▲▲
•LEVEL OF DIFFICULTY•	🚶 🚶 🚶
•PATHS•	Country lanes, woodland tracks and fields, 17 stiles
•LANDSCAPE•	Hilly, with agriculture and woodland, extensive views
•SUGGESTED MAP•	aqua3 OS Explorer 189 Hereford & Ross-on-Wye
•START / FINISH•	Grid reference: SO 630346
•DOG FRIENDLINESS•	An exciting stretch, but limited off-lead opportunities
•PARKING•	Marcle Ridge Picnic Place
•PUBLIC TOILETS•	None on route

Walk 30 Directions

Begin downhill, along a narrow lane, for about 500yds (457m). Part of the woodland on the right here was coppiced in 2001, a task long overdue. Subsequent cutting at the correct frequency will yield wood for various coppicing products, and the land will be suitable for game shooting. A fingerpost points right, down to a wood. Note how calcareous the ground is.

Geologically, the so-called Woolhope Dome is a 'denuded anticline', that is, a massive fold of limestone that has been subsequently worn away. Shallow soils make farming only the lower slopes practicable, leaving limestone-loving species to populate the ridges.

Turn right, then left before a dilapidated barn. This stony track turns left to reach **Hyde Farm** within 300yds (274m). Veer right but, within 60yds (55m), find a track going steeply uphill and back to your right (yellow waymarker).

Archaeologists believe that the number of lives lost in the 14th-century Black Death may have been exacerbated by food shortages in the two decades that preceded it: the summers, though hot, were short, lowering yields. The 'solution' was to increase the cultivated land by clearing further up the hillsides. Thus some 'ancient woodland' may only date from the post-Black Death period.

Where this woodland track bends left, go straight, over a stile. Cross most of an expansive field, finally turning half left and up, aiming for an aperture in the corner – a track into **Busland Wood**. On your right are 20th-century larches, but the latter part of the wood, an indigenous deciduous mix, has been coppiced for generations. (Several field boundaries here have been

WHILE YOU'RE THERE ℹ️

Newbridge Farm Park at Little Marcle has tractor rides, pony rides, handling of the smaller animals, a large outdoor play area and a play barn. At Much Marcle is **Weston's Cider** (visitor centre).

WHERE TO EAT AND DRINK ⓘ

Before Woolhope is the **Butchers Arms**. In Woolhope the **Crown Inn** serves Wye Valley ales, draught cider and good food.

grubbed up, which explains the sudden change of direction in the field.) Walk for 200yds (183m) in this wood, again going straight, into a meadow, where the track turns. Go ahead for 250yds (229m). Find a marker post above a small, dry valley. Swing left, to a gate into more trees. Keep on this track, steadily downhill, for about ½ mile (800m), to a tarmac lane – the **Butchers Arms** is just here. Turn left, up through downtown **Woolhope**. Just beyond a high wall find a fingerpost on the left, Cross four meadows to reach a footbridge flanked by stiles. Over this go straight ahead (not right) for about 50yds (46m), then cross a narrow lane. Cross two waymarked fields, veering right in the second to a corner gate. Turn left. Go through a gate just beyond **Alford's Mill** to a stile bearing three arrows. Turn left, over a footbridge. Follow the right-hand field edge for 130yds (119m). Turn right, over a stile.

Walk initially beside a fence. Keep this line for ½ mile (800m), later squeezing between two spinneys into lush pasture. A stile to the right of **Court Farm** soon leads to **St Michael's Church** at Sollers Hope.

Built in the English Gothic style, St Michael's Church was altered in 1887, when plaster was removed to reveal the well-preserved timbers of its barrelled roof. Also discovered was a 13th-century stone coffin lid, showing the coat of arms of the de Solers family, who owned the estate and gave the hamlet its name.

Take a stile near the main churchyard entrance to walk to the right of several modern farm buildings. Keep this direction past an orchard and across another meadow to a stone barn. Cross the lane here to walk beside a ponded stream. Maintain this line to reach another minor lane. Turn left. One bend after a stream, don't swing right on a private gravel driveway; instead go straight on, up a rough track beside **Lyndalls Wood**. Towards the top of the wood and just inside it are the remains of lime kilns. Locally quarried limestone was burnt with coppiced wood (or perhaps coal from the Forest of Dean). The oxidised product, lime, has various uses, such as making whitewash. Ascend for ½ mile (800m). Shortly before the brow turn left, up some wooden steps.

WHAT TO LOOK FOR ⓘ

Court Farm is nearly 400 years old. As you approach, you'll see an incredibly leaning **chimney pot**. A little further on, you'll see that it is, indeed, not credible – it's braced with an iron strut in the roof.

To view **Oldbury fort**, turn right here then retrace your steps. The first 'hedgerow' you come to is an earthwork delineating Oldbury's northern boundary. Some people believe that while forts such as Oldbury functioned as defensive focal points in times of need, they were built to some extent for 'show', giving its people a cultural identity, not dissimilar to the Christian 'culture' of building churches.

Having gone up the wooden steps, go straight along the ridge for nearly 1¼ miles (2km), passing close to the radio and television mast. Finally, steep wooden steps lead down to the car park.

Berrington Court: 'Back to The Fruiture'

A moderate stroll around a rural backwater, among more trees than a forest.

•DISTANCE•	5¾ miles (9.2km)
•MINIMUM TIME•	2hrs 30min
•ASCENT / GRADIENT•	280ft (85m) ▲▲▲
•LEVEL OF DIFFICULTY•	🚶 🚶 🚶
•PATHS•	Town streets, field paths, minor lanes, 15 stiles
•LANDSCAPE•	Undulating mixed farmland, small market town
•SUGGESTED MAP•	aqua3 OS Explorer 203 Ludlow
•START / FINISH•	Grid reference: SO 598682
•DOG FRIENDLINESS•	Lead preferable most of time
•PARKING•	Long-stay car park, beside swimming pool, Tenbury Wells
•PUBLIC TOILETS•	Off Teme Street and on Market Street

BACKGROUND TO THE WALK

The 'Wells' in Tenbury Wells only came about after attempts in the mid- to late 19th-century to capitalise on the mineral water in the town's wells. The Pump Rooms, built in 1862 and recently restored, are its other legacy, but it was too late into the fashion – Malvern Wells, Droitwich Spa, Buxton Spa and the like – for it to yield prolonged success.

Apples Under Threat

Once upon a time Tenbury was known as 'the town in the orchard'. It has been estimated that between 1970 and 1997, 64 per cent of Britain's orchards were grubbed up. Why? Often it was because the grants system operated by the then Ministry of Agriculture, Fisheries and Food (MAFF) encouraged many farmers to grow cereals, not top fruit. Orchards on urban peripheries were, and those that remain still are, ripe for house-building. The cider industry is still thriving – witness the number of young orchards you may see while driving in the two counties – but some varieties of apple are verging on extinction.

Fruit Tree Kits

On this walk you will notice that Frank P Matthews grows a lot of trees. The company sells about 60 varieties of apples. They also have a commercial interest in 'tree heritage', being the supplier of rare species to the Fruit Tree Kits scheme, administered by the Herefordshire Council Parks and Countryside Service and run every autumn.

The scheme's stated aim is 'to help people source old apple varieties that were once traditionally grown in Herefordshire but that are now rarely planted or difficult to obtain commercially and in turn restore or replant traditional standard orchards.' Those available may be culinary, dessert, or cider apples. A particularly quirky apple is called Ten Commandments; this is a rather insipid dessert apple, in fact, but its strange name comes from its bizarre internal colouring – when cut open, ten red spots are evenly spaced around its core. The scheme is not exclusively for apples, embracing particular varieties of quince, plum and pear.

Commercially, apple trees are propagated by grafting on to another rootstock. One reason for this is that they might otherwise grow into large but relatively unproductive trees. The time of maturing, the 'cropping capacity' and the final height of the tree are therefore determined by the rootstock on to which it is grafted. The fruit tree kits for orchards are supplied on rootstock coded 'M25', that is a vigorous sapling that will grow to a standard height of perhaps 33ft (10m). However, to widen the net of propagation, fruit tree kits can also be purchased for growing in a garden. Trees for this purpose are 'M26, dwarfing', growing to 8–12ft (2.4–3.6m) tall, making them practical for the gardener to harvest.

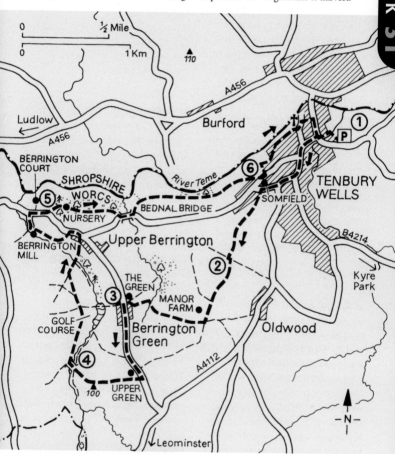

Walk 31 Directions

① Leave the car park by the 'no exit' sign. Over the bridge with railings turn left. At the **Crow Hotel** turn right then immediately left. Now walk through Tenbury Wells. Cross over beyond **Pembroke House**, soon taking 'Berrington'.

Opposite the bungalow, **Somfield**, cross a stile. Go up and down to another, walk on level ground, following power poles. Cross a ditch over planks behind fallen trees. Go to the field top.

② Turn left then right. Cross fields to join the driveway of **Manor Farm**. About 50yds (46m) beyond

Walk 31

a bridge turn right at a triple waymarker to a close stile. Cross fields for 440yds (402m). Veer down and right, through a gap, then back up left, and through **The Green**'s several gates.

③ Go left on this lane for 750yds (686m). Some paces past '30mph' follow the unsigned driveway of abandoned **Upper Green**. Through more gates, head for the far left field corner. Start up the left edge. Over the brow, at an old tree line, strike diagonally, to a footbridge.

WHERE TO EAT AND DRINK ℹ

Despite its modest size, there are plenty of options in Tenbury Wells, including a pizza house. In the heart of Tenbury is the **Crow Hotel**, which has a beer garden. Several of its pubs are old, timber-framed affairs, including the **Royal Oak** in Market Street, the **King's Head Hotel** in Cross Street and, on the route out, **Pembroke House**, which serves Caffrey's Irish Ale.

---

④ Turn right, soon on Cadmore Lodge Hotel's **golf course**. Go straight and level, leaving the course when a little beyond the hotel. Walk round the right field edge, then down a farm track. Join a minor road between imposing dwellings. Turn left. In 100yds (91m) take the fingerpost, up some steps. Cross this field diagonally. A path leads through bracken to **Berrington Mill** (and many high-decibel dogs). Turn right, up the lane, then right to Frank P Matthews' nurseries at **Berrington Court**.

⑤ Take the track behind a house. Enter the nursery. Walk beside mind-boggling numbers of potted trees under glass (or plastic). Leave this gravel track where it cuts down through woodland. Meadows lead

---

WHILE YOU'RE THERE ℹ

About 3 miles (4.8km) south east of Tenbury Wells is **Kyre Park**, a large private house, basically medieval with Elizabethan and Jacobean pieces bolted on, set in 32 acres (13ha) of landscaped gardens, including five lakes, a medieval dovecote (resited in 1756), and a brick tithe barn from 1618. You can get married here if you want to, or just share a pot of tea. Apart from running about in the gardens, children have a 'fun palace' and there's even a miniature soft play area for toddlers.

---

to **Bednal Bridge**. Just beyond it take double gates into trees. Keep your line when this ample track runs out. It's now straightforward to the outskirts of Tenbury. (A yellow arrow pointing right eases a sharp slope.) Round the backs of gardens, emerge through a gate.

⑥ Turn left, but only for 15yds (14m). Take a hedge-hugging kissing gate, on the left. Now go forward, across the flood plain, for 90yds (82m). Turn right (a gate aperture is now behind you) to hit suburbia again. Turn left. Move left at 'No cycling'. Keep on the tarmac footpath, left of No 14, soon beside tall garden fences. Emerging at the church, turn left. Opposite a church gate turn right, down **Church Walk**, to **Teme Street** and thence your car.

WHAT TO LOOK FOR ℹ

No 18 Teme Street (now the Country Restaurant) once housed Tenbury's most famous resident, yet he lived there for less than a year, struck down by tuberculosis when aged 30. Henry Hill Hickman, born in 1800, was a pioneer of anaesthetics, but never a practitioner (and only recognised posthumously), beyond experimenting with animals. The seventh of a farmer's 13 children, he was a truly brilliant youth.

The Historic City of Hereford

A walk around a medieval city that still retains some of its ancient charm.

•DISTANCE•	2¾ miles (4.4km)
•MINIMUM TIME•	1hr 45min
•ASCENT / GRADIENT•	Negligible
•LEVEL OF DIFFICULTY•	
•PATHS•	City streets, riverside path and tracks
•LANDSCAPE•	Riverside and city
•SUGGESTED MAP•	aqua3 OS Explorer 189 Hereford & Ross-on-Wye
•START / FINISH•	Grid reference: SO 510403
•DOG FRIENDLINESS•	Not great for dogs, off lead beside river possibly
•PARKING•	Garrick House long-stay, pay-and-display multi-storey car park, Widemarsh Street
•PUBLIC TOILETS•	Blueschool Street, Castle Green, East Street and elsewhere
•NOTE•	Several busy junctions without subways – care needed

BACKGROUND TO THE WALK

The city of Hereford is small enough for market day – Wednesday – to be discernibly busier than other weekdays. This is currently less obviously the case, as its agricultural economy claws its way back from being slaughtered by the foot and mouth disease episode in 2001. Hereford has a shrinking steel business, and relies heavily on the food industry – Sun Valley (chicken meat products) and Bulmers (cider) – and on you, the visitor. Sun Valley sponsor Hereford United football team. Bulmers, who put brand awareness above parochial sentiment, currently pay Leeds United to play with Strongbow emblazoned on their shirts. Neither of these firms employs as many in the city as the Herefordshire Council, the most recent administrative mutation. The county-corporate logo is a perfect green apple – a conservative choice. The apple may no longer be economically supreme, but it is indubitably more politically correct than a headless chicken – such a choice would certainly have ruffled a few feathers.

History and Architecture

Despite the presence of a munitions factory at Rotherwas, the city was essentially unscathed during the Second World War. Visually, like most other shire towns, Hereford's latter 20th-century development was largely unpleasant – the Inland Revenue building in Broad Street and the encroachment of the Tesco supermarket into the city wall at the Edgar Street roundabout are particular horrors. However, Hereford retains pockets of charm, several of which our route embraces. The city oozes history – its castle site, its cathedral, the Mappa Mundi, and so on. The six-arched Wye Bridge, built in 1490 and strengthened in 1626, has seen a lot of traffic, vehicular and military. It was a focus of fighting in the 1640s, when the city changed hands several times. It has enjoyed relative tranquillity since 1965, when its ugly big sister was built. Beside the Wye Bridge, the recently completed Left Bank project – the biggest development since the Maylord Orchards shopping precinct in the 1980s – has really made a difference to this quarter of the city. (It's a mystery why the windowed buttress is not of the same local sandstone colour as the massive retaining wall.)

On the walk, take the opportunity to detour south, down Broad Street, to see the tall, honey-and-grey City Library, which also houses the art gallery and museum; currently deemed 'inadequate' for its functions, it was built in a Gothic style, with quite elaborate carvings. Also down here is the Roman Catholic St Xavier's Church – you can't miss its custard-coloured, Greek Doric columns – threatened with demolition in the 1990s. Until current refurbishment is complete, Mass is being held in Hereford Cathedral on Saturday evenings and in All Saints on Sunday mornings.

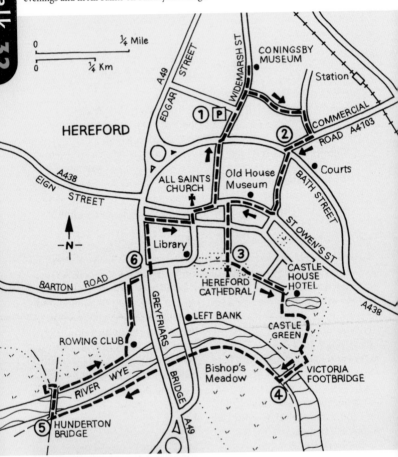

Walk 32 Directions

① Turn left out of the car park. Within 150yds (137m) is the Coningsby Hospital built in 1614 (now **Coningsby Museum**). Go back a little way to walk along industrious **Coningsby Street**, to a T-junction. Turn right, along **Monkmoor Street**, noting that

Canal Road points to the site of the triple canal basin terminus of the Hereford and Gloucester Canal, now the yard of a builders' merchant. Turn right into **Commercial Road**, where the Litten Tree occupies a former warehouse. At the **Blueschool Street** junction on the far side is more city wall, while on the near side are the shiny new magistrates' courts.

② Cross first **Commercial Road** then **Bath Street**. Follow **Union Street**, then go right to **High Town**. Go left down narrow **Church Street**, to **Hereford Cathedral** (to the right of which is the tourist information centre).

③ Go left, beside the cathedral, passing the stonemasons' workshop. Go along **Castle Street**. Shortly before the **Castle House Hotel** turn right to **Castle Green**. Hug the railings on the left, beside **Castle Pool** (part of the original moat), to walk above the green and its Nelson Column (1809). Zig-zag down to cross **Victoria Footbridge**.

> **WHERE TO EAT AND DRINK** ℹ
> The place to be seen sipping coffee nowadays is the **Left Bank** complex. The sandwiches at **Ascari's**, on the corner of Berrington Street and West Street, have a high reputation. The **Moka Bar** at No 8 Church Street can be quite a crush – always a good sign – and at No 10 is the **Sandwich Bar**. Near by too is **Nutter's Wholefood Coffee Shop**.

④ Turn right (or left for an extended riverside stroll), passing the putting green, tennis courts and a wood carving. Keeping on the south side of the river – opposite the regenerative **Left Bank** complex – cross **St Martin's Street** to go under **Greyfriars Bridge**, continuing to **Hunderton Bridge**.

⑤ Cross this old railway bridge. When the River Wye floods, blocking the roundabout south of the city, this popular footway and cycleway provides emergency vehicular access. Take steps down to head back towards the city. (Walk 40 touches our route here.) Skirt the rowing club, then walk up **Greyfriars Avenue**. Just before the

> **WHILE YOU'RE THERE** ℹ
> Only devout heathens avoid **Hereford Cathedral**; this, and the **Mappa Mundi** and **Chained Library** (entrance fee) are the biggest draws. A circular, three-dimensional **model** of the hills around Hereford, on the City Library's porch wall, will interest walkers. Mounted on the stair wall is a stunning Roman mosaic floor from nearby Kenchester. On Bishop's Meadow you'll find an endangered species, municipal grass tennis courts – use them or lose them.

junction go half right across a car park to go through a pedestrian subway. (But go right, through the car subway, to see a large chunk of the city wall.) The brick building immediately in front of you is built directly on the city wall. Up some shallow steps, cross **St Nicholas' Street** with utmost care.

⑥ As you begin along **Victoria Street**, see a solitary tree. A few paces beyond it, about 10ft (3m) up in the city wall, is a cannon ball, supposedly embedded there during the siege of Hereford in 1645. Go along **West Street** to **Broad Street**. Turn left. Walk towards **All Saints Church** – does its tower lean backwards? Turn right but then left, down **Widemarsh Street**, back to your car.

> **WHAT TO LOOK FOR** ℹ
> Visit the **Old House Museum** (open Tuesday to Sunday, April to September) in High Town. A three-dimensional model depicts 17th-century Hereford. Near by is the relocated Marchants' House. Near the cathedral, the sign 'Tower open today' means you can climb the cathedral's stairs (most days in school summer holidays). Due to be unveiled in 2004 is Hereford's latest piece of art, a sculpture of Edward Elgar – a snip at £30,000.

Walk 33

Beside the River Wye and up Coppet Hill

This peaceful walk in a popular corner of Herefordshire includes an energetic climb, rewarded with fine views.

•DISTANCE•	6¾ miles (10.9km)
•MINIMUM TIME•	3hrs
•ASCENT / GRADIENT•	855t (260m) ▲▲▲
•LEVEL OF DIFFICULTY•	🚶 🚶 🚶
•PATHS•	Quiet lanes, riverside meadows, woodland paths, 2 stiles
•LANDSCAPE•	Much-photographed river valley
•SUGGESTED MAP•	aqua3 OS Explorer OL14 Wye Valley & Forest of Dean
•START / FINISH•	Grid reference: SO 575196
•DOG FRIENDLINESS•	Good, but dogs forbidden in castle grounds
•PARKING•	Goodrich Castle car park open daily 9:30AM to 7PM
•PUBLIC TOILETS•	At start

BACKGROUND TO THE WALK

The well-preserved remains of Goodrich Castle seen today are of building work carried out in the 12th and 13th centuries, replacing those from the early 12th century. Some gory traps and ruses kept would-be intruders away. The most often quoted is a tunnel beneath the gate tower that could be blocked by a portcullis; doomed attackers would then be scalded with hot water from above or, better still, burned to death with molten lead (presumably recyclable).

Ghost Story
The castle eventually succumbed to Parliamentarians in 1646 during the Civil War, led by Colonel John Birch, who had successfully attacked the city of Hereford the previous December. The story goes that the colonel's niece, Alice, and Charles Clifford, her lover, fled from the battle, only to meet their deaths trying to cross the River Wye. So watch out for their ghosts on a phantom horse. Goodrich Castle is open daily from 10AM to 5PM, except between November and March, when the opening days are Wednesday to Sunday, and the hours are 10AM to 1PM and 2PM to 4PM.

A Simple Price
The oddly named Welsh Bicknor was once a detached parish of Monmouthshire. Welsh Bicknor Youth Hostel is just one of approximately 225 in England and Wales. The Youth Hostels Association (YHA) began with 73 buildings, many donated, in 1931. The organisation arose to meet the increasing demand from ramblers, cyclists and, in particular, youth organisations for simple, inexpensive accommodation. The YHA has, in relative terms, remained true to this concept, but it has also moved with the times – some would say too slowly, others would say too quickly – improving the quality of its accommodation in line with the relentlessly rising expectations of the recreational public. It seems cherished by the minority that uses it, yet overlooked (inexplicably?) by the majority that doesn't.

The YHA was rocked by the closure of the countryside during the 2001 foot and mouth episode. Not only did it lose an estimated £5m in revenue, but individual hostels, run with considerable autonomy, were ineligible for financial assistance as 'small businesses' because of their association with the central organisation – to maintain its cash flow the YHA had to put ten youth hostels up for sale.

On Location

The area around Symonds Yat has, in recent years, attracted film buffs who wanted to see the locations used for Richard Attenborough's film, *Shadowlands*, the stars of which were Debra Winger, Anthony Hopkins and Symonds Yat. The film was based on the life of C S Lewis, author of *The Chronicles of Narnia*.

Coppet Hill Nature Reserve is managed by a trust. It earned Local Nature Reserve status in 2000 after 14 years of conservation management.

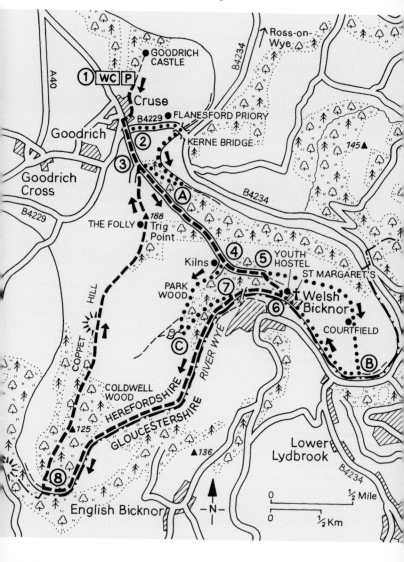

Walk 33 Directions

① Walk back to the castle access road junction and turn immediately left. In 125yds (114m) cross a bridge over the **B4229**.

② Go up a further 400yds (366m). Ignore another road branching off to the right, and go on just a few paces – there are three low wooden posts to your left.

③ Opposite, between the two roads, a sign 'Coppet Hill Nature Reserve' indicates your return route. Go another long ½ mile (800m) up this dead end, to reach a cattle grid. Here, at the brow, the woods end, giving way to parkland. Go straight ahead for another 275yds (251m) to a solitary horse chestnut tree at a right turn.

> **WHAT TO LOOK FOR** ⓘ
> Just 100yds (91m) from Point ④ are some partly covered **kilns**, marked by a clump of trees growing on top. As you climb Coppet Hill, notice much formerly **coppiced woodland**, where the trees were 'let go' when the demand for coppice wood petered out.

④ Keep ahead for another 400yds (366m), bending left and dipping down, the road once again tree-lined. The road curves right a fraction, while a gravel track goes up a ramp and fractionally left.

⑤ Curve right. Ignore the pillared driveway – 'Courtfield' and 'The Mill Hill Fathers' – but go down the youth hostel's driveway. At its entrance gate take a footpath that runs initially parallel to it. Descend wooden steps and a sometimes muddy path to a T-junction beside the **River Wye**.

⑥ Turn right, following the **Wye Valley Walk** (turn left to visit the church first). Within ¼ mile (400m) you'll reach an old, iron girder railway bridge, which now carries the Wye Valley Walk across the river, but stay this side, passing underneath the bridge. In about 125yds (114m) look for six wooden steps down to the left at a fork.

> **WHILE YOU'RE THERE** ⓘ
> For a river cruise, try **Kingfisher Cruises** at Symonds Yat East, where you'll also find the **Saracen's Head** (a former cider mill) and the hand ferry. **Jacqueline 'O' River Cruises** are at Symonds Yat West, where you'll also find the **Amazing Hedge Puzzle** maze.

⑦ Take the steps, to remain close to the river. (The right fork is where Walk 34 rejoins for the final time.) Continue for about 1¼ miles (2km). Enter **Coldwell Wood** to walk beside the river for a further ¼ mile (400m). On leaving, keep by the river in preference to a path that follows the woodland's edge. In about 350yds (320m) you'll reach a stile beside a fallen willow.

⑧ Turn right, signposted 'Coppet Hill'. Soon begin the arduous woodland ascent. Eventually you'll have a fine view. The path levels, later rising to **The Folly**, then goes down (not up!) to a triangulation point. Follow the clear green sward ahead, becoming a narrow rut then a stepped path, down to the road, close to Point ③. Retrace your steps to the castle car park.

> **WHERE TO EAT AND DRINK** ⓘ
> A **kiosk** in the castle car park serves hot drinks, soup, jacket potatoes and cakes. **Jolly's of Goodrich** is the village store and post office. The **Hostelrie Hotel** serves coffee, tea and lunchtime bar food.

Around Coppet Hill

This extension leaves and rejoins the main route no fewer than three times!
See map and information panel for Walk 33

•DISTANCE•	9¾ miles (15.7km)
•MINIMUM TIME•	4hrs 45min
•ASCENT / GRADIENT•	1,215ft (370m) ▲▲▲
•LEVEL OF DIFFICULTY•	👥 👥 👥

Walk 34 Directions
(Walk 33 option)

At Point ② on Walk 33 descend the bridge's steps to pass **Flanesford Priory** (little remains of the original 14th-century Augustinian priory). After the pavement, walk briefly on the verge to **Kerne Bridge** (1828). Take a stile on the right. After entering trees, follow the Wye Valley Walk for another 400yds (366m), to a signpost, 'Goodrich 1 mile', Point Ⓐ. Take this path, emerging at three wooden posts, Point ③. Follow Walk 33, noting Point ④ but continuing to Point ⑤.

Take the track past a sign, '10mph through works' (where are the works?). This hard track is dead straight for ½ mile (800m), then curves very gently down, behind **Courtfield**, a manor house. At a 'Private' sign keep the high wall to your right.

Courtfield Estate belonged to the Catholic Vaughn family, but in 1651 the land was confiscated. It was only in the late 18th century that the majority was returned. Courtfield is now the St Joseph's Retreat Centre, home to the Mill Hill Fathers, a Catholic order.

The track ends one field before the River Wye. Descend to the river, Point Ⓑ. Turn right, along the bank, for over ½ mile (800m). Just beyond the YHA's landing stage you'll enter the church grounds.

Although **St Margaret's Church** combines Norman and Early English styles, it was built as a whole in 1858–9. The ruin beside it, seemingly a farmhouse, contains a decaying cider mill and press.

A few paces past the youth hostel is a waymarker – this is Point ⑥ on Walk 33, but do not rejoin that route. Instead turn right, up the wooden stepped path. At the gate join the driveway, to walk past Point ⑤ back to Point ④. Facing **Goodrich**, turn left. In 300yds (274m), when green fencing on the left ends, fork left.

After larches and a cattle grid before a new house, fork left, down to gates just beyond overhead cables, Point Ⓒ. Take the left-hand gate, turning sharp left, so passing under the cables again. Continue downhill, along the outside edge of **Park Wood**. Reach a gate into woodland, beside a horse fence. To rejoin Walk 33, go through this gate. Pass a squat stone ruin, soon reaching the riverside at Point ⑦.

Kyrle-on-Wye

An easy perambulation, enjoying the legacy of a Ross philanthropist.

•DISTANCE•	3¼ miles (5.3km)
•MINIMUM TIME•	1hr 45min
•ASCENT / GRADIENT•	330ft (100m) ▲▲▲
•LEVEL OF DIFFICULTY•	林 林 林
•PATHS•	Suburban streets, woodland and riverside paths, no stiles
•LANDSCAPE•	Classical town built on hill overlooking river
•SUGGESTED MAP•	aqua3 OS Explorer 189 Hereford & Ross-on-Wye or OL14 Wye Valley & Forest of Dean
•START / FINISH•	Grid reference: SO 582239
•DOG FRIENDLINESS•	Limited off-lead opportunities
•PARKING•	Car park on B4260 between Wilton Bridge and Ross-on-Wye
•PUBLIC TOILETS•	In town

Walk 35 Directions

Find a Wye Valley Walk board at the back of the car park, behind the skate-boarding area. Cross the footbridge to take the upward path, initially just slightly left (quite steep). At a junction, turn very sharply right on a level path, called The John Kyrle Walk, just a few paces before a multiple waymarker.

It's as hard to avoid the name John Kyrle in Ross-on-Wye as it is to avoid William Shakespeare in Stratford-upon-Avon. Kyrle (1637–1724) was a wealthy man, though not stinking rich. He studied law but didn't qualify. From his early 20s he lived a frugal lifestyle, generous with his money and, more importantly, the type of person who 'made things happen'.

After about 500yds (457m) go through a gate and descend some steps to a hollow. Turn left. This becomes a tarmac path, emerging

by a house called **The Cleeve**. Turn left. At a road go straight across, continuing on a path beside houses. Keep on this alleyway as it crosses several residential streets, to reach the disused railway line. Turn left. Follow this, decorated with trees and occasional picnic tables, to a junction on the **B4234**. Cross over to take **Fernbank Road** (off Eastfield Road). Keep straight ahead, ignoring Woodmeadow Road. The road becomes a track, rising steadily, entering **Chase Wood**.

Turn left just before the buildings of **Hill Farm**, through a gate on a descending path. After about 30yds (27m) take the larger, left fork, to

WHILE YOU'RE THERE ⓘ

Occupying the prime centre spot, you should go inside the **Market Hall**. Before returning to your car, go a little further along the riverside to **Wilton Bridge**. Built in 1597, it was strengthened with concrete ties in 1914. A public footpath circumnavigates the remains of nearby **Wilton Castle**.

Walk 35

soon descend on a stepped path. At the bottom reach a T-junction. Turn right. At a gate turn left, following a right-hand field edge. Cross the railway again. An alleyway becomes a cul-de-sac. Turn right into **Merrivale Lane** but cross immediately to a narrow alleyway beside an electricity sub station. Turn right. Keep on the tarmac when it turns left. At the end of this road (**The Avenue**) turn right, then immediately left into **Ashfield Crescent**. Next take the first right then, at a skew crossroads, go along **Redhill Road**. Pass **Ashfield Park Avenue** and the primary school. Turn right at a crowd of waymarkers. (Here you are not many paces from a point on the outward walk.) Take the fenced path beside the school's playing fields. Shortly you'll reach the large churchyard. At the wall of **The Prospect** turn left to enter it through the 1700 gateway. The Prospect is perhaps the most tangible legacy left by John Kyrle – a place for relaxation, and, most important at the time (1696), a fountain providing a ready supply of water to the townsfolk.

> **WHAT TO LOOK FOR** ⓘ
> The architectural historian Pevsner called the Italianate **Baptist chapel** in Broad Street 'very terrible', yet its architect, G C Haddon, also designed the chapels at Dulas (► Walk 41) and Ewyas Harold.

Leave The Prospect by the gateway close to **St Mary's Church**. John Kyrle was buried in the chancel here. To date, historians have failed to find any blemish upon his character; the nearest thing to it seems to have been having to go to a petty court for failing to remove a dung-heap from outside his house – it isn't known whether the horse was his.

Leave the church grounds by the main entrance, passing the fine, sandstone **Rudhall's Almshouses** (1575). Turn left into **Church Street**, then right at a T-junction, to reach the **Market Hall** and, opposite it on the right, John Kyrle's house. Retrace your steps up **High Street**, passing the end of Church Street. Stay on High Street until its end. (The tourist information centre is just on the right-hand corner here.) From this junction walk perhaps 70yds (64m) along **Wilton Road** to see the stone gazebo (formerly Collins' Tower, after its owner), then return to the junction.

> **WHERE TO EAT AND DRINK** ⓘ
> Ross-on-Wye has plenty of pubs, tea rooms and restaurants. On the walk are the **Man of Ross**, above the river, and the **Hope and Anchor**, beside the river.

The 1830s was a period of great activity in Ross, sparked by the 1830 Improvement Act (which primarily addressed sewage and drainage). The gazebo, together with the nearby Royal Hotel, dates from 1837, when large amounts of the red sandstone were hacked away from the modest cliff to build what is now Wilton Road.

Now pass in front of the **Man of Ross** public house (the plaque in front of it describes the 18th-century problems of muddy streets). Descend steps to reach the river beside the **Hope and Anchor** pub. Turn left. (Here the wheel for pumping water up to the town once stood.) Follow the tarmac path when it turns left. Go through the white bollards and across the road. Go diagonally across the grass to the pedestrian subway – this leads back to the car park.

Aymestrey: Quarrying the Rocks of Ages

What have 'Capability' Brown, Richard Payne Knight and Hanson Aggregates got in common? Find out on this brief walk through time.

•DISTANCE•	4¾ miles (7.7km)
•MINIMUM TIME•	2hrs 30min
•ASCENT / GRADIENT•	525ft (160m) ▲▲ ▲▲ ▲▲
•LEVEL OF DIFFICULTY•	🚶🚶 🚶🚶 🚶🚶
•PATHS•	Excellent tracks, field paths, minor roads, steep woodland sections, 11 stiles
•LANDSCAPE•	Wooded hills and undulating pastures
•SUGGESTED MAP•	aqua3 OS Explorer 203 Ludlow
•START / FINISH•	Grid reference: SO 426658
•DOG FRIENDLINESS•	Several opportunities for controlled, off-lead walking; lead needed on two stretches of lane
•PARKING•	At old quarry entrance, on east side of A4110, ¼ mile (400m) north of Aymestrey Bridge
•PUBLIC TOILETS•	None on route

BACKGROUND TO THE WALK

On your way here, you may have seen signs to the village of Shobdon and the adjacent Shobdon Airfield. It was one of the many airfields built in 1940, as part of what was collectively perhaps the biggest civil engineering project undertaken in Britain. At that time a modest, privately owned quarry was operating at Aymestrey. The wartime government used its compulsory purchase powers, ensuring a local supply of stone for the airfield. In its latter years the quarry was run by Hanson Aggregates.

I don't suppose that anyone at Hanson Aggregates expects, in the fullness of time, to be remembered for their landscape architecture in the same way as the ubiquitous Lancelot 'Capability' Brown, or Richard Payne Knight (▶ Walk 37), but they should at least be commended for trying.

Landscape Continuum

Unfortunately you will not be best placed to judge the quality of their 'seamless' landscape restoration, since I've already primed you to look out for it. Nevertheless, towards the end of the walk, as you descend to the former quarry area, there is little to indicate that the immediate landscape has been recently manufactured, although your curiosity may be alerted by the absence of any really substantial trees. Unlike many quarries, the plan here was not to provide any sort of lake-based recreation, but to return the land to a mixture of agricultural use (sheep grazing, it seems) and woodland.

In geological time, man's quarrying is scarcely a moment. Unfortunately, working out a quarry can take up a fair amount of a person's lifetime – people tend not to like quarries in their backyards, so quarries often get a bad press. The quarry companies will argue that 'restoration' and 'environmental sensitivity' were among their objectives a decade or two before their current fashionability, and that, far more often than not, sand and gravel quarries are returned to a level of agricultural utility that at least equals the one before.

Glacial Gorge

West of Aymestrey the River Lugg runs in a small but spectacular gorge. This is a glacial overflow channel that exploited a fault in the rock, associated with the glacial Wigmore Lake. The paucity of contours on the suggested map a few grid squares to the north shows the position of the former lake. At Mortimer's Cross, Richard of York's son Edward defeated the Lancastrian army in 1461 in one of the battles that changed the course of the Wars of the Roses (Edward was crowned King later that year). The battle site is ½ mile (800m) south of the road junction named Mortimer's Cross. The cross itself dates from 1799.

Walk 36 Directions

① Walk up the access road for almost ½ mile (800m), until beyond the garden of a new-ish house and

just before a junction of tracks. Note a stile on the right – your route returns over this.

② Go 30yds (27m) further and turn left, passing a seemingly

nameless house with a stone wall relic in its garden. Continue, through **Yatton**, to a T-junction. Turn left to the **A4110**. Cross directly to a stile, walking along the left-hand field edge. Through a gate go forward then skirt round the right edge of an oak and ash embankment, to find a corner stile. Walk up the left edge of this field but, at the brow, where it bends for some 70yds (64m) to a corner, slip left through a gap in the hedge to walk along its other side. Within 60yds (55m) you will be on a clear path, steeply down through woodland, a ravine on your left. Join the driveway of **River Bow**, to a minor road. (The glacial overflow channel is directly ahead.)

> ### WHILE YOU'RE THERE ⓘ
> You'll have to do this walk on a Thursday if you want to visit **Lucton Mill** (also called Mortimer's Cross Water Mill), managed by English Heritage. Remarkably, this 18th-century mill was still grinding corn commercially in the 1940s. The wheel still turns today from time to time. You could spend the best part of a day on the **Croft Estate** – as well as viewing the castle, there are waymarked walks.

③ Turn left here, joining the **Mortimer Trail**. Enjoy this wooded, riverside lane for nearly ¾ mile (1.2km), to reach the **A4110** again. Cross, then walk for just 25yds (23m) to the right. (The **Riverside Inn** is about 175yds/160m further.) Take a raised green track, heading for the hills. Then go diagonally across two fields, to a stile and wooden steps.

④ Ascend steeply through the trees. Leave by a stile, to cross two meadows diagonally. Take the stile on the right to walk along the left-

> ### WHERE TO EAT AND DRINK ⓘ
> At Aymestrey Bridge (over the River Lugg) the **Riverside Inn** brews its own Woodhampton Ales. Here you can eat anything from simple baguettes to proper country fare, including local black pudding and apple compôte, lamb's kidneys and saddle of rabbit. The **Mortimer's Cross Inn**, at the junction of that name, has a beer garden and a children's play area.

hand edge of a field, still heading downhill. At the trees turn left. Soon reach a tarmac road. Turn left along the road, now going back uphill. Beyond **Hill Farm**, enter the **Croft Estate**. Walk along this hard gravel track. After 110yds (100m) ignore a right fork but, 550yds (503m) further on, you must leave it. This spot is identified by an end to the deciduous trees on the left and a Mortimer Trail marker post on the wide ride between larches and evergreens on the right.

⑤ Turn left (there is no signpost). Within 110yds (100m) go half right and more steeply down. This aged access track gives expansive views over felled forest. Within 250yds (229m) look out for a modern wooden gate, waymarked, leading out of the woods. Walk along its right-hand edge (and beside a recently appended small plantation). At the far corner, within the field, turn left to Point ②. Retrace your steps to the start of the walk.

> ### WHAT TO LOOK FOR ⓘ
> As you walk through Yatton there are stunning brick-arched **barns** on the right. These tall stone structures have brick apertures; one is filled in with attractive gridded brickwork. Later, look back from the other side of the A4110 to see more arches.

Walk 37

Picturesque Downton Castle

A long stretch in a landscape designed to please the eye.

•DISTANCE•	10 miles (16.1km)
•MINIMUM TIME•	4hrs 30min
•ASCENT / GRADIENT•	1,200ft (100m) ▲▲▲
•LEVEL OF DIFFICULTY•	👫 👫 👫
•PATHS•	Pastures, leafy paths, grass tracks, dirt tracks, tarmac lanes, 13 stiles
•LANDSCAPE•	Rolling country, wooded and farmed, above River Teme
•SUGGESTED MAP•	aqua3 OS Explorer 203 Ludlow
•START / FINISH•	Grid reference: SO 403741
•DOG FRIENDLINESS•	Mostly on lead, lots of game birds
•PARKING•	Community centre and village hall car park, Leintwardine
•PUBLIC TOILETS•	At start (not always open)

BACKGROUND TO THE WALK

By the end of the 18th century, formal neatness in landscape architecture had fallen out of fashion; the new word on the lips of those who counted was 'picturesque'. This craving for a more 'laissez faire' type of landscape had been of great benefit to Ross-on-Wye (► Walk 35), where the Wye Tour had become the must-do trip for everyone who was anyone. Downton on the Rock was to benefit from Richard Payne Knight, under whose direction Downton Castle was built between 1772 and 1778. If you like regimented rows of trees, twee fountains, manicured lawns, symmetrical paths and so on, then Downton Castle is not for you.

Richard Payne Knight

Extensive tree planting would have occurred around the time that the castle was built. Richard Payne Knight knew exactly what sort of landscape he wanted, having travelled extensively, particularly in Italy. He sought a rugged, wild view. It is believed that Payne Knight had been influenced by the landscape paintings of Nicolas Poussin (French), Claude Lorrain (French) and Salvator Rosa (Italian), who had produced their best works in the mid-17th century. Poussin had worked at the Louvre in Paris as painter to the king, whereas Lorrain and Rosa had studied in Naples. None came from privileged backgrounds and all had struggled to gain recognition for their work. For some time after they had established themselves as artists, all three lived as near neighbours in a little street in Rome called Trinità dè Monti. It would be interesting to compare their works with those of the little-known English painter, Thomas Hearne, who painted several views of the Downton Estate. Incidentally, the British landscape painter, John Constable, was born in 1776, when Downton Castle was being built. It is said that, when aged about 20, sight of a particular painting sparked Constable's smouldering ambition to be an artist – the French masterpiece he saw was *Hagar and the Angel*, by Claude Lorrain.

As for the privately owned Downton Castle's interior, it is wholly classical in style. Some alterations and additions were made in the 1860s. The best view of the castle is to be seen from Castle Bridge.

Roman Leintwardine

The Romans built a fort beside the River Teme here, and stayed at Leintwardine until the late 4th century AD. Where an early church is found within a Roman earthwork, the inference is that usage of the site continued when the Romans left, as is the case with Leintwardine. The High Street lies on the line of the Roman Watling Street. Today Leintwardine's population is well below half its late 19th-century figure of nearly 2,000.

Walk 37 **Directions**

① Walk through Leintwardine to **Watling Street**. At the primary school turn right. Go half left at a stile. In an orchard remnant, curve left. Avoid a private drive. At a road turn right, along tarmac. In 300yds (274m) turn left, to the **A4113**. Cross, turning immediately right up a lane. Ascend for a short mile

(1.6km). Soon after a skew junction go forward. Cross three fields, into woodland. At the A4113 turn left but soon right, beside a wire fence. At the end follow the field edge round to the left for 70yds (64m). Go down an earthy bank (on your bottom?) in trees to pass stables on your right, then along a good dirt road, soon dead straight for ½ mile (800m) to **Brakes Farm**.

② Go straight ahead (waymarker). Cross a minor road diagonally, then cross fields to a minor lane beside houses Nos 20 and 19. Turn left. Soon turn right, downhill. Turn right, along the river, just before **Forge Bridge**. Skirt two unnamed houses. Up a bank, join a substantial track. Follow this to **Castle Bridge**. Ascend but within 110yds (100m) of leaving woodland go half right. Rejoin the track into forest for perhaps 60yds (55m). Scramble up a bank (waymarker). Traverse the steep meadow to a gate in the top, among oaks. Keep this line to go down a wide meadow, locating a stile into trees.

③ Turn left and descend. When you reach open meadow, curve round a dry valley. At a left bend go through a gate on the right. Go left of a specimen oak to a hidden stile in the bottom corner. Cross over a footbridge and turn right. Cross meadow to a gate, and soon reach a minor road. Turn right. Descend

easily through **Burrington**, to its church. Behind the church, cross meadows to **Burrington Bridge**. Cross the **River Teme**. After 650yds (594m) take the right turn. When you reach **Downton**, head towards **Old Downton House,** but then turn left. Beyond a wall take the rightmost gate (waymarker), along an old lane. Ascend a right-hand field edge, later following a beech-lined avenue to reach a junction with a dirt track.

WHERE TO EAT AND DRINK ⓘ

There are no refreshments on the way, but you could finish with this convenient sequence – moisten your lips in the **Sun Inn**, a simple parlour bar, satiate your appetite and replenish your salt levels at the **fish and chip shop**, close to the village green, and finally wash it down with another drink in the riverside beer garden of the **Lion Hotel**.

④ Over a stile, descend, initially steeply. Past a small pond veer left along a right-hand field edge. Turn right. After 120yds (110m) of road go through a difficult gate with a discouraging notice. In the bottom left-hand corner of this field find a stile just beyond power lines. Veer right (but cross a drainage ditch) to another stile. Aim for houses ahead. Pass through two gates. On the residential road turn left, then right. Back in **Leintwardine**, turn right at the **Lion Hotel** and return to the start of the walk.

WHILE YOU'RE THERE ⓘ

At 24 Watling Street is **Peter Faulkner**, a coracle maker. A coracle is a rudimentary, lightweight oval boat, made from interwoven branches of willow and usually hazel, with an animal skin or cotton cloth, coated with pitch, stretched over its base. Coracle, as river craft, are believed to pre-date the Romans.

WHAT TO LOOK FOR ⓘ

At **St George's Church**, Burrington, are several iron slab tombstones, among which is that of 'Richard Knight, MDCCXLV' (1745). He was the grandfather of Richard Payne Knight, who had purchased the Downton Estate with money earned from his life as one of the Shropshire ironmasters.

Walk 38

Kilpeck and Orcop Hill

A walk once enjoyed by a young woman who became a wartime heroine.

•DISTANCE•	4¾ miles (7.7km)
•MINIMUM TIME•	2hrs 45min
•ASCENT / GRADIENT•	590ft (180m) ▲▲ ▲▲ ▲
•LEVEL OF DIFFICULTY•	🚶🚶 🚶🚶 🚶
•PATHS•	Field paths, tracks and minor lanes, 21 stiles
•LANDSCAPE•	Wooded, grazed and cultivated hills
•SUGGESTED MAP•	aqua3 OS Explorer 189 Hereford & Ross-on-Wye
•START / FINISH•	Grid reference: SO 445304
•DOG FRIENDLINESS•	Good, on-lead exercise, not allowed in Kilpeck churchyard
•PARKING•	Spaces beside St Mary's and St David's Church, Kilpeck
•PUBLIC TOILETS•	None on route

BACKGROUND TO THE WALK

The bottom of a garden seems an odd place for a museum, but the Violette Szabó, GC Museum is a very personal one. It stands in the grounds of Cartref, the modest house to which Violette Szabó would come to visit her cousins. Rosemary Rigby, who lives there now, is both the museum's creator and curator. Among the many attending the museum's opening in 2000 was Violette's daughter, Tania.

Violette Bushell had a French mother and an English father. When Violette was 11 they moved to London. Violette met Etienne Szabó, a Hungarian-born French national 12 years older than she, at London's Bastille Day Parade in 1940. After a whirlwind romance – not uncommon in wartime – they married 41 days later. In February 1942 Violette gave birth to Tania, whom Etienne was never to see, for he succumbed to chest wounds inflicted in the Battle of El Alamein that October. Seeking revenge, Violette joined the Auxillery Territorial Service (ATS), from where she was head-hunted by the French section of the Special Operations Executive (SOE). Her second mission on the ground in France was to be her last.

Among the museum's exhibits is a door of the car believed to have been the one in which Violette Szabó, Jacques Dufour (the local Maquis leader) and a friend of his had been travelling to visit another Maquis member when they encountered a Nazi road block. In the ensuing gun battle her two companions escaped, uninjured, but Violette had to surrender when she ran out of ammunition. She was – posthumously – awarded the George Cross, the first woman to be honoured in this way. Although unaware of major Nazi troop movements, it isn't clear why Dufour, who was driving, decided to take on the soldiers at the road block, rather than turning the car round and hoping they wouldn't be pursued, or at least hoping to find a better escape route, for example, but this was the beginning of the end.

From her capture on 10 June 1944 until her execution on 28 January 1945, Violette was moved eight times, enduring rape, brutal assaults and inhumane living conditions, particularly at Ravensbrück concentration camp and three months at Königsberg on the Russian Front. The outcome could have been so different. Alerted to where Violette was being held, two SOE colleagues intended to rescue her from Limoges Prison, which wasn't heavily guarded. Tragically, just hours before they planned to do it, she was moved to Fresnes Prison in Paris.

Of the SOE's 55 women members, 11 were killed in service, either in France or in concentration camps. R J Minney's biography of Violette Szabó was published in 1956. In the 1958 film, *Carve Her Name with Pride*, Virginia McKenna – who attended the museum's opening – portrayed Violette. Although Steve Tomlinson's summary account of Violette Szabó's life, available at the museum, doesn't dwell on Ravensbrück's horrors (where 92,000 women died), it still leaves a grim memory of a fanatically and remorselessly cruel regime.

Walk 38 Directions

① Walk down to the **Red Lion**. Turn right. At the junction follow 'Garway Hill'. Take the second

fingerpost. Find another stile behind **The Knoll** (house). Strike diagonally across pasture. Cross another stile, now with the field boundary on your right. Veer left to reach a lane at a bend. Turn left.

Follow waymarkers through trees, then go straight down a field to near a junction.

② Turn left, past **Two Brooks**. After 500yds (457m) turn left, through a gate by **Grafton Oak**, tucked behind. Soon in a scenic meadow, follow the fence until a crossing stile. Now keep ahead but drift down, guided by a gigantic oak. The stile you need is ahead, not another, further down, that crosses a brook. Contour with trees on your left for two fields. In the third find a footbridge down and left.

③ Follow waymarkers, diagonally up the field. Walk with a wire fence on your right. Leave this long field at its top end (but, to observe rights of way, first cross and re-cross the wire fence on your right, via a wooded area). Go diagonally to an opening beside a hollow oak, not the more easily seen, three-bar stile. Move left to walk along the left-

WHERE TO EAT AND DRINK

At Wormelow Tump, on the A466 and close to the museum, is the **Tump Inn**, just reward for those who have made it there on foot. It has a beer garden, a children's play area, bar meals, snacks and an Italian restaurant. Happily, the **Red Lion** at Kilpeck stands just two minutes from the end of the route, an ideal spot for well-earned refreshment.

hand field edge. Ignore a waymarker into the left-hand field – any way out has completely disappeared. Instead keep straight, to a tarmac road. Turn left. After 650yds (594m) a fingerpost slants left. (Walk 39 leaves here.)

④ Take this path through bracken to a track. Turn right for 25yds (23m), then left, to pass to the right of **Saddlebow Farm**. The avenue below leads into a field. Walk along this right edge, to just before another gate. Join a very good track, following it for 650yds (594m), until three gates in a corner.

⑤ Take the second on the left. Beyond **New House Farm** go over ¼ mile (400m) to a junction. Don't turn down to Kilpeck yet! Go 160yds (146m) further. Here go left, around some old farm buildings. Descend to an unseen gap not 50yds (46m) left of the bottom right-hand corner. Out of this copse, cross two fields to pass between the buildings of **The Priory**. An avenue of horse chestnuts leads to the **Red Lion**.

WHAT TO LOOK FOR

People flock to **Kilpeck church** to look at the large number of decorated corbels that adorn the building's exterior. As Norman churches go, it is one of the best preserved in England. It was probably built at the same time as a former Benedictine Priory – 1134. Beside the church is a substantial motte and bailey, also 12th-century. Part of this has been absorbed into the churchyard. There are vestiges of an enclosure, roughly 200yds (183m) by 300yds (274m), defining a Saxon village here.

WHILE YOU'RE THERE

Visit the **Violette Szabó, GC Museum**. Add a quick and easy 3½ miles (5.7km) to Walk 39 from Point ©. Walk away from the ponds, curving round to The Mynde's iron front gates. Turn right, past the lake. Now just keep going on waymarked driveways and tracks for nearly 1½ miles (2.4km). At the A466 go diagonally left – the museum is 275yds (250m) down the lane. It is open on Wednesdays, 11AM–1PM and 2–4PM, April to October, but please telephone in advance should you wish to visit outside these times.

Orcop Hill – a Longer Walk

Enjoy the views for longer, with an opportunity to go on foot to the Violette Szabó, GC Museum (► While You're There).
See map and information panel for Walk 38

•DISTANCE•	7 miles (11.3km)
•MINIMUM TIME•	3hrs 45min
•ASCENT / GRADIENT•	950ft (290m) ▲▲▲
•LEVEL OF DIFFICULTY•	🏃 🏃 🏃

Walk 39 Directions
(Walk 38 option)

From Point ④ keep on the road for nearly ½ mile (800m). Beside **Butts Bungalow** take a delightful track, ascending in **Mynde Wood**. After 300yds (274m) in the woods find a waymarked stile, Point Ⓐ.

Grubbing out has made this a huge field. The next stile is 400yds (366m) away, well left of the line of the steepest slope. Turn left on to a green motorway. At the T-junction turn left. Over the crest, drop steeply but only half-way: a stile just after a grassy cattle grid enables you to skirt **Bettws Court Farm**. Re-ascend. About 60yds (55m) beyond a protruding corner take a stile into Mynde Wood once more, Point Ⓑ.

Descend steadily. Leave the wood for a paddock. Go right of the brick-floored stables to a track, then turn left, beside a house. Through the gate ahead, turn right. Temporary fencing for horses makes the way unclear. You can use the next gate ahead, then go right, into and out of the rusty-red corrugated shed (which garages an old fire engine), take a gate on the

left and turn right. Standing on a well-made dirt road, with **The Mynde** to your right and two ponds to your left, you are at Point Ⓒ.

From the outside The Mynde is imposing yet bland, its rendered finish detracting from any embellishments. Inside, it apparently has a very large hall, but none of the privately owned building, in part 16th-century, is open to the public.

Go past the ponds, following this road for over ½ mile (800m). Just before the minor road it bends right – go straight on, hugging the left field edge, to pass a modern house to your right. Cross this road and the next field. At a woody corner go down, left, to cross a stream. Now go half-right and a little up to a low metal gate. Strike across this large field, neither gaining nor losing height for the first 200yds (183m) then, veering left a fraction, descend steadily to cross a stream. Go up again, to reach a minor road beside **Nash Hill Cottage**. Cross this, into another field. Go diagonally for 60yds (55m) then straight down the slope for two fields. At a ditch go three-quarters left, to cross two more fields and emerge in **Kilpeck** village beside the **Red Lion**.

Hereford's Percy and Fred

Catch a bus from Hereford for this linear walk beside orchards and the Wye.

•DISTANCE•	3¾ miles (6km)
•MINIMUM TIME•	1hr 45min
•ASCENT / GRADIENT•	82ft (25m) ▲ ▲ ▲
•LEVEL OF DIFFICULTY•	🚶 🚶 🚶
•PATHS•	Farmland and woodland paths, old railway bed, 9 stiles
•LANDSCAPE•	Orchards, arable fields and riverside pastures
•SUGGESTED MAP•	aqua3 OS Explorer 189 Hereford & Ross-on-Wye
•START•	Grid reference: SO 471414 (city bus stop SO 503401)
•FINISH•	Grid reference: SO 503400 (Cider Museum)
•DOG FRIENDLINESS•	Some arable fields, but many cattle beside Wye
•PARKING•	At Cider Museum (patrons only); or city centre
•PUBLIC TOILETS•	None on route but several in city
•NOTE•	Catch First 101 bus (every 15 minutes) from nearby Eign Street towards Credenhill and ask for 'Wyevale Nurseries'

Walk 40 Directions

From the bus stop opposite Wyevale Nurseries on the **King's Acre Road** take the signed public bridleway between beech hedges. It's straight. Eventually cross a farm track to put a hedge on your left. At the end of **Wyevale Wood** cross a stile. In adjacent modern orchards one substantial oak stands defiantly.

By the time you reach these orchards the bus you caught will be in Credenhill, home of the founding brothers of H P Bulmers, Percy and Fred. Their father was rector at Credenhill for several decades, and was also a contributor to the *Herefordshire Pomona*, a tome on apples. In 1887, having completed a history degree at Cambridge, Fred joined his brother in preference to taking up the opportunity to tutor the King of Siam's sons. It was some time before steam power eased the physical effort of cider-making. At

the start both brothers worked a 16-hour day for much of the year, either walking the 4 miles (6.4km) home to save the rail fare or sleeping overnight at their workplace. On the latter occasions, the suppers their mother had cooked for them would be taken by a boy on the train from Credenhill to Hereford.

Use two stiles to cross a tarmac road. Keep on this line with a hedge on your left, eventually to reach, in a corner, a kissing gate (Wye Valley Walk marker). Sheep graze in the traditional orchard on the left. Within 60yds (55m) cross another road at **Breinton Court Lodge**. Go diagonally across a disturbed orchard then a car park corner to a

---

WHILE YOU'RE THERE ⓘ

Visit the **Cider Museum**, allowing enough time to do it justice. The child-friendly **Waterworks Museum** combines the history of drinking water with the engineering of Victorian steam pumping engines (check for opening times).

kissing gate. Here head straight across (leaving the Wye Valley Walk). Under some power lines cross a new-ish fence. Keep this diagonal to a green path that passes to the right of the churchyard, reaching a kissing gate. Atop a wooded embankment, initially skirting the vicarage's vast garden, walk beside more grazed orchards.

WHAT TO LOOK FOR ℹ

From the riverbank you'll see the Waterworks Museum's Italianate **water tower**. In the city look for the number plate 'C1 DER' on the car driven by the preceding years' most successful sales rep at Bulmers.

The Bulmer brothers' business stuttered early on when the local apple crop was so poor, because of wet weather, that they had to buy their raw material expensively from Somerset. The turning point came when, having filled new, large storage tanks with cider in a year of good harvest, they were able to sell all their stocks at a premium price after a bad harvest two years later.

Direct mail – or 'junk mail' – is not a new concept. Bulmers were one of the earliest to apply this method of creating demand – press and poster advertising was considered too costly. After a day of physically arduous work the brothers would spend their evenings poring over directories, to cull names and addresses of landed gentry, peers, the clergy and doctors, then sending out circulars to this 'target audience'. According to Fred's account, this effort meant that after some years they had accrued 20,000 customers, a big enough base for them to become a 'wholesale only' company. Bulmers' Woodpecker brand was first sold in 1896.

Beyond these orchards a stile leads into an open field. Soon look for a new metal kissing gate that puts the hedge on your left, in pasture. Some 60yds (55m) beyond a massive plane tree, turn right to join a muddy track down to the **River Wye**. Turn left. Follow the river bank for 1½ miles (2.4km), as far as the old railway bridge.

As a child, Fred Bulmer suffered so badly from asthma that he did not go to school. During this school-less childhood he taught himself French. When the business blossomed he went on a visit to France, where the cider-makers of Epernay gave him advice and colleagues demonstrated their *méthode champagnoise* – perhaps their descendants now rue that generosity.

First published in 1937, and written in the style of the period, *Early Days of Cider Making* by Edward Frederick Bulmer is a delightful read, a genuine story of sweat, endeavour, opportunism and good fortune – it even has a wicked godfather. The book is available from the Cider Museum.

At the old railway bridge ascend steps to turn left – beware of whizzing cyclists! Go along this old railway trackbed. Abruptly, just beyond a road bridge, this sylvan cyclepath and walkway spills into Retail Britain. Wade across the huge supermarket car park to find the seemingly diminutive **Cider Museum**, ahead and to the left.

WHERE TO EAT AND DRINK ℹ

At No 69 St Owen Street is the **Barrels and Wye Valley Brewery**; at No 88 is the **Victory** pub and Spinning Dog Brewery. The **Café at All Saints** is a café in a church that's moved with the times.

Delights of Abbey Dore

In search of a 19th-century workhouse in the glorious Golden Valley.

•DISTANCE•	8 miles (12.9km)
•MINIMUM TIME•	3hrs 45min
•ASCENT / GRADIENT•	540ft (165m) ▲▲▲
•LEVEL OF DIFFICULTY•	🚶🚶 🚶
•PATHS•	Meadows, tracks and woodland paths (one stony, awkward descent), 24 stiles
•LANDSCAPE•	Quintessential Herefordshire
•SUGGESTED MAP•	aqua3 OS Explorer OL13 Brecon Beacons (East)
•START / FINISH•	Grid reference: SO 386302
•DOG FRIENDLINESS•	Mostly on leads, can run on common if no sheep
•PARKING•	On east side of B4347, south of lychgate, facing south
•PUBLIC TOILETS•	None on route

BACKGROUND TO THE WALK

You may find yourself sipping tea in the conservatory of the Abbey Dore Court Garden. There is no particular history attached to the present building, but it stands on the site of the former Red Lion public house. Here, in 1837, took place the inaugural meeting of the Board of the Dore Union Guardians, and weekly meetings for two years thereafter. It was their job to commission, construct, and manage a workhouse in the locality. The unworkable law, under which each parish was meant somehow to cope with its own poor, had been replaced by the Poor Law Act. Thus the 'Union' was a group of 29 parishes. Another facet of the 1834 legislation was compulsory provision of schooling for workhouse children. At that time there were five workhouses within the bounds of Hereford City, one of which subsequently served as part of the County Hospital. Right up until its demolition in 2002 the building still bore the stigma, among elderly people, of having been 'a poorhouse', raising their reluctance to be admitted to it.

Poverty Within

'Riverdale', as the Dore workhouse buildings are marked on the map today, is a remote place, well away from Abbey Dore itself, which has never been a metropolis. The most disliked rule, and perhaps the least necessary, was the one that forbade 'inmates' to leave the premises. The rules of the workhouse – in fact, taken from one in Hereford – were strict but not Draconian; criminal acts were rare. Breaches were often punished by reducing diet (but such punishment could not be given to children). The diet's key elements were bread, gruel (an inferior porridge, of oatmeal and water) and potatoes. Five ounces of meat per person were allowed two days per week and one-and-a-half ounces of cheese on four days per week. One wonders if they might have been more productive had they eaten more! Most of the residents were aged or infirm; many had additionally suffered some other misfortune: blind persons, abandoned wives, unmarried mothers, and so on; and many in the workhouse were children.

In 1929 legislation transferred responsibility for residents of poorhouses to county councils. During the Second World War the Dore workhouse was used for tractor assembly.

The buildings were subsequently converted into a modest number of private dwellings, but in the height of their workhouse days they had accommodated between 80 and 100 men, women and children, reduced to 68 in the 1870s. Nevertheless, the physical conditions inside the workhouse may have been little worse, if at all, than those of many agricultural workers living within its 29 parishes, who endured the discomfort of damp and cramped cottages without a solid floor.

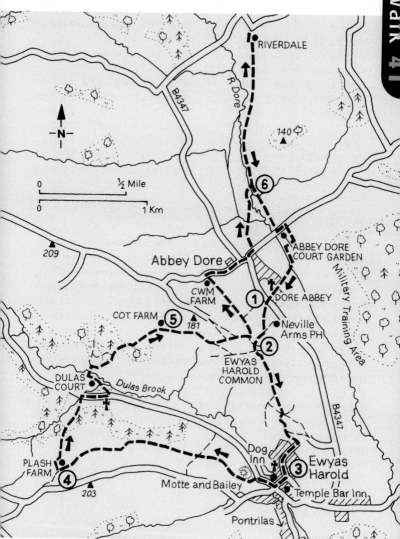

Walk 41 Directions

① Cross the **B4347** at the lychgate. Slant left up fields. Beside a dwelling go up a path, to a third field, then a corner stile. In 20yds (18m) turn right up a hedged lane to **Ewyas Harold Common**.

② This is the prescribed route but dozens of paths and tracks crisscross here. Across the immediate concrete track take the left diagonal ride. In 65yds (60m) take the slightly left option. After 45yds (41m) bear right. In 325yds (297m) take the right-hand option. After 70yds (64m) move left slightly to resume your line. In 160yds (146m) move 10yds (9m) left on a wide track, then turn right. In 55yds (50m) turn left on a big gravel track. Just beyond a seat fork right, down a rutted track. After a cluster of three houses swing right, over a cattle grid.

WHERE TO EAT AND DRINK ⓘ

Ewyas Harold has the **Temple Bar Inn** and the **Dog Inn**, a bar, bistro and free house. In Abbey Dore the **Neville Arms** serves cask ales (and fine meals). At **Abbey Dore Court Garden** tea rooms, tea and wonderful cakes are served in the courtyard or the conservatory.

---

③ Down in the village, turn right then right again. At the sharp bend ascend some steps. Aim left of a spinney. After old buildings ascend three fields, finding a corner stile. When the trees end, swing up and left to a boundary corner. Keep field edges on your right, to **Plash Farm**.

④ Get behind the farmhouse by turning right twice. Go down to the bottom corner. A sunken lane leads to a road. Turn right, then left to **Dulas Court**. Cross the brook by a bridge beside new buildings. Turn right in 30yds (27m). Go diagonally up the meadow into conifers. Walk

uphill for 50yds (46m) to a track, but, within 30yds (27m), a clear path bears right, uphill. Out of woodland, aim for a pole, then pass between the buildings of **Cot Farm**.

⑤ Walk with a hedge on your left. Keep this line across fields, to regain the common. In 70yds (64m) join a track (left part of the hairpin), then 70yds (64m) further go straight ahead on a green sward, soon joining another track. Some 50yds (46m) before a house, which you should recognise from earlier, turn left. Stiles over deer fences lead to the lane by **Cwm Farm**. Turn right. Before **Abbey Dore Court Garden** find a stile at a tiny bridge. In the third field after 300yds (274m) move right to cross a bridge.

⑥ Waymarked stiles lead to **Riverdale**. Retrace your steps to Point ⑥. Now keep on the east side of the river. Turn left at the road. In about 60yds (55m) take a well-waymarked route between the military fence and the gardens. Finally, a concrete footbridge, a meadow and an agricultural graveyard lead to the abbey.

WHAT TO LOOK FOR ⓘ

Beyond Ewyas Harold a spinney conceals a Norman **motte and bailey**, with a maximum height of 42ft (13m). Looking east, over the rooftops of the abbey, is a stationary **train**. Resting where the railway has been disused for 45 years, it is used as military training equipment.

WHILE YOU'RE THERE ⓘ

Aside from the scenery, it's primarily **Dore Abbey** that draws people to this part of Herefordshire. Originally part of the great Cistercian abbey, much of it was built between 1175 and about 1220. It was restored and re-roofed as a parish church by the somewhat philanthropic Viscount Scudamore in the 1630s; he also added the tower. The roof is currently (2003) being re-tiled using local sandstone. In Ewyas Harold **St Michael's Church**, apart from being a fine building in its own right, contains a 13th- or 14th-century effigy of a lady holding her heart in her palm.

Hergest Ridge at a Trot

Rise up from a market town to a glorious ridge overlooking Wales.

•DISTANCE•	7½ miles (12.1km)
•MINIMUM TIME•	3hrs 30min
•ASCENT / GRADIENT•	1,115ft (340m) ▲▲▲
•LEVEL OF DIFFICULTY•	🚶 🚶 🚶
•PATHS•	Meadows, field paths, excellent tracks, 14 stiles
•LANDSCAPE•	Panoramas on Hergest Ridge
•SUGGESTED MAP•	aqua3 OS Explorer 201 Knighton & Presteigne
•START / FINISH•	Grid reference: SO 295565
•DOG FRIENDLINESS•	Sheep country and some horses
•PARKING•	Mill Street car park (east and west sides of Crabtree Street)
•PUBLIC TOILETS•	On Mill Street

BACKGROUND TO THE WALK

This is not the hardest walk in this book, but the first thing you need to know is that 'Hergest' rhymes with 'hardest'.

The suggested map shows 'Race Course (disused)' along Hergest Ridge. It was a focus of entertainment from 1825 to 1846. It had replaced the one on Bradnor Hill (north of the town), first used in the 1770s. Racing stopped round about 1880, but being up on the hill must have given considerable relief from the nauseating stench of the town's surface sewage. The Hergest Ridge section is one of several highlights for walkers undertaking the Offa's Dyke Path. The path and the ancient earthwork itself often do not coincide, but that doesn't seem to matter – they still represent a mighty piece of history and a fine long distance route. Adjacent to Bradnor Hill is Rushock Hill, and a particularly well-preserved section of the Offa's Dyke that the National Trail route follows – you will have to make a separate excursion on foot to see it.

The industrial estate that straddles the road south west of Hergest Bridge stands on the site of a 'camp', a wartime military hospital, dilapidated parts of which remain. Closer to the town, on the opposite side of the road to the toll house, the (almost) level field served as a landing strip – all 300yds (274m) of it!

KC3 – The Kingston Connected Community Company

Kington was essentially a wool-trading market town, on an important drovers' route. St Mary's Church was certainly visible from afar, a tall spire on a hilltop position. The Norman tower had to be rebuilt in 1794. The remainder was built later, mostly 13th-century, with Victorian additions. A small market town on the Anglo-Welsh border seems an unlikely place for 'cutting edge' technology, which is precisely why KC3 exists at all. Now ten years since its inception, it was a synthesis of private and public money (Apple Computers, British Telecommunications, the Rural Development Commission and the then Department of Trade and Industry). Its purpose was to see if and how information technology could be applied to regenerate a declining rural economy and rejuvenate the community. The company now stands on its own feet financially, and claims to subsidise its community activities. It's near the library, on the corner of High Street and Bridge Street.

Walk 42

Hergest Court

Hergest Court was once one of the many properties owned by the Vaughan family. Vaughan's wife's brother had been murdered, for which she effected revenge in dramatic fashion. Dressed as a man, she attended an archery contest where her brother's killer was, and despatched him with a fatal arrow. She then fled. Sir Thomas Vaughan was killed in the Wars of the Roses. Their alabaster effigies lie in Kington's St Mary's Church. Beside the recreation ground stands Lady Margaret Hawkins School – much changed and expanded, it's been a school since 1625.

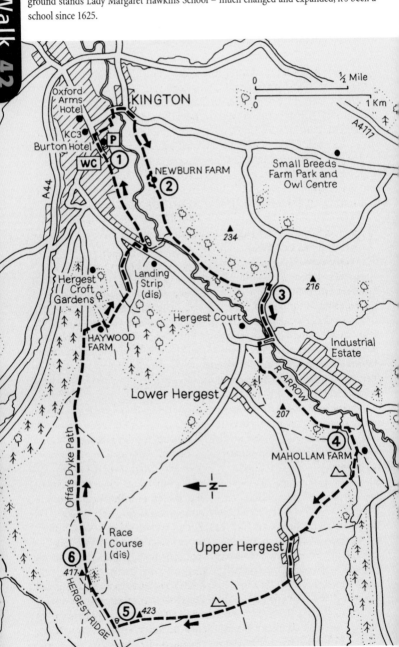

Walk 42 Directions

① Walk down the **High Street**. Take an alley on the right, between a hairdresser and a menswear shop. Zig-zag to **Bridge Street**. Turn right. Cross the **River Arrow**. Take the driveway to **Newburn Farm**.

② You are invited to walk through the farmyard. Go round three sides, then take a gate into a field. After an area planted with trees (including cherry and ash), don't be drawn down. Take a stile to a right-hand field edge, under huge oak limbs. Walk for over ½ mile (800m) through meadows, curving left to a stile and steps down to a road.

③ Turn right. Turn right again to cross **Hergest Bridge**. After 100yds (91m) take a left fingerpost. Along the right field edge, cross a stile into trees. On a track, bend left. Cross a meadow to a line of sweet chestnuts. Over a difficult stile, turn right, along an awkward path across a steep, wooded bank. After 325yds (297m) a stile puts you into another meadow. Cross a footbridge. Drop slightly to skirt woodland and reach a marker post. Cross two more stiles in this imperfect pasture. Go ahead and fractionally right for 80yds (73m) to a single-plank stile and a waymarker (possibly obscured).

Another, more substantial, double-stiled footbridge stands 40yds (37m) ahead. Bear left, to find, in 100yds (91m), steps down to a metal footbridge.

④ At a road on a caravan site for seasonal farm workers turn right. Just 30yds (27m) after some gates find a stile (perhaps overgrown), right. Almost immediately, take a second stile beside a huge oak. At a track beside **Mahollam Farm** bear right, downhill. Do not stay on this green lane, but go right, finding another substantial metal footbridge. Ascend steeply, soon in farmland. Cross fields to an old road. Turn right. Go left for 400yds (366m), to a gate. Now go straight up to the trig point on **Hergest Ridge**.

⑥ A clear path leads to a pool. Turn right. Now stride out for 1½ miles (2.4km). On the road again, when 30yds (27m) beyond a sign proclaiming 'Kington – the centre for walking', turn right. Round **Haywood Farm**, continue down to a cattle grid. Down this road look for a fingerpost beside the white 'No 31'. Go down this field. Turn away from Kington for 120yds (110m), then turn sharply left, '16 Tatty Moor'. Cross meadows to the recreation ground. Join **Park Avenue**, which becomes **Mill Street**.

Harley's Mountain Air

This bracing walk in a corner of Herefordshire is just what the doctor ordered.

•DISTANCE•	3¾ miles (6km)
•MINIMUM TIME•	2hrs 15min
•ASCENT / GRADIENT•	755ft (230m) ▲▲▲
•LEVEL OF DIFFICULTY•	👫 👫 👫
•PATHS•	Meadows, field paths, woodland tracks with roots, 10 stiles
•LANDSCAPE•	Wooded hillsides and farmland, views to higher Welsh hills
•SUGGESTED MAP•	aqua3 OS Explorer 201 Knighton & Presteigne
•START / FINISH•	Grid reference: SO 364672
•DOG FRIENDLINESS•	Horses near Lingen but few sheep; exciting woods
•PARKING•	At St Michael's Church, Lingen (tuck in well)
•PUBLIC TOILETS•	None on route

BACKGROUND TO THE WALK

After the Second World War the nascent European Economic Community devised the well-intentioned Common Agricultural Policy (CAP) to address food shortages. This 'good idea' did not embrace the diversity of farming conditions, practices and cultures, and could not foresee subsequent technological advances. In its later years the CAP fell into disrepute – its supporters might say because it was so successful – because surpluses resulted, and maintaining these perishable stores was costly. The scheme was also contentious because many of the larger players in the global food market, in particular the United States, were jumping up and down, saying (correctly, it seems) that exportation of such surpluses was illegal because they arose from subsidised production.

Set Aside

It was therefore deemed necessary to reduce the European output – 'set-aside' was introduced in the 1992 CAP reforms. Under the scheme, farmers essentially left some fields 'unfarmed' and received financial compensation for loss of income. That such a scheme was completely contrary to the traditions, instincts and ethics of many in the farming community was overlooked.

Set-aside was still running in 2001, when farmers were obliged to leave 10 per cent of their food acreage out of food production. The payment (or 'compensation') received was partly dependent upon which side of the Welsh border your land lay. In England the rate was £88 per acre (£218 per hectare) but in Wales it was £77 per acre (£190 per hectare). Set-aside land could be used for growing 'industrial' as opposed to food crops. Set-aside land could be either part of a crop rotation or left for successive years. In environmental terms, favoured fields would be those adjacent to existing hedgerows, copses, commons and the like.

The latest 'radical' change to the way in which the European Union manages its agriculture was floated in 2002. The crux of the new strategy is to cut the link between the quantity a farm produces and the size of the subsidy it receives, instead making fixed, one-off payments based on historical values, and making payments for 'environmental services'. This goes down well with environmentalists – who say that the United Kingdom has the 'fastest rate of birdlife diversity loss in the EU' – since it removes the financial incentive to intensify farming. In its simplest form, the argument runs that a sheep farmer who is paid per sheep will put as many sheep on the land as possible, leading to overgrazing and consequent erosion and loss of biodiversity. However, if the small-scale hill farmer is happy with the money side of it, this does not insure against environmental degradation – encroachment by forest, bracken and the like – owing to undergrazing. Clearly the solutions to the agricultural economy will continue to tax policymakers for years to come.

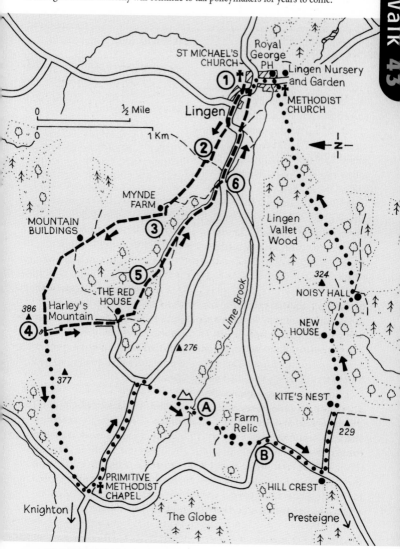

Walk 43 **Directions**

① Walk away from the **church** and cross over to take the minor road signposted 'Willey'. When you reach the first bend, follow the fingerpost directly ahead. Climb over a difficult gate beside a small corrugated shed, then walk by the paddock edge, reaching a little-used lane in trees.

② Strike up the field, passing a dead oak. Follow a waymarker up and slightly right. In the corner, negotiate the rusty gate between better ones. At the derelict **Mynde Farm** skirt left, around two collapsed buildings. Find a gate on the right behind a low building still standing.

③ Go down and up a wide meadow to a stile seen from afar. Veer left, passing beside **Mountain Buildings** on a deeply rutted, rocky track. Some 160yds (146m) further, enter a large field. The line you require is diagonally across the field (but if ridged with potatoes, for example, follow two field edges left); then keep that line, now with a hedge on your left. Take the track along this breezy ridge to a gate with a small pool to the right (possibly dry in high summer). Above and behind you is the dull, grey trig point. (Walk 44 leaves here.)

④ Turn left, initially preferring the left-hand field edge to the lane, here overgrown. Descend steadily for 650yds (594m). At the bottom move left, down to a small gate. Through trees, shortly emerge close to **The Red House**. Go dead ahead, finding a narrow path within trees, right of the garage and beside a hedge. Within 40yds (37m) negotiate a metal gate. Do not be tempted down; instead move left, beside a wire fence for just a few paces, then, maintaining that fence's line, proceed to walk below a narrow

ridge on a faint green tractor track for perhaps 100yds (91m). When the ground ahead drops steeply into a dell turn half left, to walk down the woody edge of a meadow. In the second meadow, where the trees bulge out to the left, dive back into the woodland – a waymarker on an oak is reassuring.

> **WHILE YOU'RE THERE**
> Cross into Wales and visit nearby delightful **Presteigne**. It is surely only the border that keeps it out of the Black & White Villages Trail. Its main street is strewn with black-and-white buildings. The Judge's Lodging in Presteigne is a hands-on illustration of life and its social strata in the 1870s. A few miles south east is **Shobdon Airfield**, one of many built during the Second World War. For a different perspective on north Herefordshire, try a flight in a light plane or microlight.

⑤ Go steadily ahead, sometimes boggy, in woodland then lush pasture, for ½ mile (800m). At a wobbly silver-grey gate drop left 10ft (3m) to a waymarked stile into a once pollarded, streamside lane. Reach a road.

⑥ Turn left. After 450yds (411m), on a bend, go straight down the field to a hedge beside some farm buildings. Find a stile in that left corner. Go ahead, to another stile that gives on to the village road – take care! Turn right to view the church before reaching your car.

> **WHERE TO EAT AND DRINK**
> Lingen's pub, the **Royal George**, has fine ales from Wye Valley Brewery, and a beer garden (no dogs in the bar). Lunchtime snacks are only available at weekends. The tea rooms at **Lingen Nursery and Garden** are open from Easter to September, whereas the nursery is open from February to October; all are closed on Tuesday and Wednesday. If visiting Presteigne you'll find several options, for example, the 1616 **Radnorshire Arms** and the **Bull Hotel**. Close by, looking incongruous in a black-and-white building, is a **Chinese take away**. There's a fish and chip shop too, which also sells veggie burgers.

Upper Lime Brook Valley

Take this longer, upland route for extensive views into the Welsh hills.
See map and information panel for Walk 43

•DISTANCE•	7½ miles (12.1km)
•MINIMUM TIME•	3hrs 45min
•ASCENT / GRADIENT•	1,080ft (329m) ▲▲▲
•LEVEL OF DIFFICULTY•	👥 👥 👥

Walk 44 Directions (Walk 43 option)

At Point ④ go straight ahead, not left, for over ¾ mile (1.2km). Crossing arable fields and pastures, descend to reach a minor road. Turn left for 120yds (110m), then left, signposted 'Lingen', soon passing the diminutive **Primitive Methodist chapel** of 1862. Over ½ mile (800m) further turn right at a T-junction. Now in just 70yds (64m) take a fingerpost right, across a field to a stile, and down into the valley. Veer a fraction right, but don't be misled by sheep tracks – pick your way down this, at times inordinately steep, pasture, to find a double-stiled footbridge in a boggy patch to the right of some massive ash trees, Point Ⓐ.

Scramble up a short, wooded bank to walk with a field boundary on your left for about 250yds (229m), taking a deeply rutted farm track into a miniature valley with tall trees. Here ignore an option to fork right on a track, instead swinging left alongside an old, square-wire fence. However, in just 80yds (73m) do swing away from the fence, to pass through a gap beside a defunct stile, to the left of some dilapidated,

rusty, corrugated iron buildings. Walk 100yds (91m) diagonally left to a working stile. Walk up the left side of the field to a minor road, Point Ⓑ.

Turn left, along the road, for 650yds (594m). Turn left at **Hill Crest**. Just past a large metal barn at **Kite's Nest** take a track between hedges, not into a field. When **New House** is on your left take the lower, better-defined track, into pleasant woodland. At **Noisy Hall** initially keep just within the trees, on a narrow path close to pasture on your right. This goes deeper into woodland but after 600yds (549m) a stile gives on to meadows. Two fields later go into trees again, for a gently descending track. (At a stile and gate, a large oak has grown around a gate bar.) This becomes a deeply sunken, barrel-like lane between meadows once more. This ends at a dirt track to the public road, beside the Methodist church. Turn left through the village, then the lychgate to **St Michael's Church**.

> **WHAT TO LOOK FOR** ⓘ
>
> In Lingen **St Michael's Church** has attractive 19th-century wooden shingles on its bell-turret. On the slopes of Harley's Mountain, notice how the eroded farm track has a bed of rock, illustrating how shallow the soil is.

A Wander from Weobley

A pretty black-and-white village is the focus for this pleasant amble.

•DISTANCE•	5 miles (8km)
•MINIMUM TIME•	2hrs 15min
•ASCENT / GRADIENT•	164ft (50m)
•LEVEL OF DIFFICULTY•	
•PATHS•	Minor lanes, meadow paths, village streets, 19 stiles
•LANDSCAPE•	Gentle farmland and orchards, village
•SUGGESTED MAP•	aqua3 OS Explorer 202 Leominster & Bromyard
•START / FINISH•	Grid reference: SO 401517
•DOG FRIENDLINESS•	Leads needed on lanes and preferred in fields
•PARKING•	Village car park (signposted)
•PUBLIC TOILETS•	Beside museum in Weobley, on B4230

Walk 45 Directions

Begin by perusing the map in the car park as you may find it useful for exploring the village later. Also, you can speculate on the function of the quirky little building to your left, within the car park. Not only does it have a brick base but, above the doorway, the 'white' cladding is over more brickwork.

After a heavy snowfall Weobley is at its blackest-and-whitest, taking on an almost surreal, monochrome guise. In the spring it's inspiring, in the summer it's beautiful, and in the autumn it's simply exquisite. And I've never been to Weobley in the rain.

Opposite the car park entrance is an exemplary medieval black-and-white property, but instead of diving into the village turn left, then left again, towards the **Church of St Peter and St Paul**. It has a Norman south doorway, parts of the chancel are 13th-century, and the tall tower is from the 14th century.

Walk round two sides of the church lane, then go straight ahead on a dirt track. Keep on this track at a cluster of gates. At a single gate take a stile to cut through a traditional orchard, then walk down the left side of a huge field, later guided by power poles. Turn right to walk, fenced in, beside a lane. At the T-junction go right, on a tarmac lane beside a Bulmers' orchard planted in 2000. In the hedgerow, at regular intervals, 'standards' have been planted. The unseemly bits of plastic bag tied to these trees are to ensure that the hedge-cutter does not chop their heads off!

After 275yds (251m) take a stile into this orchard. In perhaps 60yds (55m) is a massive oak – walk just

20yds (18m) beyond this, to a
waymarker on a chest-high pole.
This points you diagonally left,
through the orchard, then two fields
bring you to a minor road. Turn
right for nearly ¾ mile (1.2km),
through the hamlet called **Weobley
Marsh**, where you may see horses
grazing on the common. Pass a red
telephone box then, 50yds (46m)
after **Link Cottage**, take the stile,
left. Over the next stile turn right,
not ahead, then cross a two-plank
footbridge to walk beside **Stone
House**. Follow its driveway to a
T-junction. Turn left for 100yds
(91m). Turn right (or continue
for barely 200yds/183m for the
Marshpools Inn). Follow the left
field boundary to another minor
road. Turn right, then left at the
T-junction. At the 'Give way' turn
left, but in just 30yds (27m) turn
right, through a strip of woodland,
into **Garnstone Park**; very little
remains of Garnstone Court. Now
go 650yds (594m) along this gravel
track to a gate and stile. Here take
the right diagonal yellow marker
(not ahead), aiming for the flakily
whitewashed far end of a long, high
brick wall. Turn right here on
another dirt track, keeping ahead
when it bends right.

At the next gate don't go through
but turn left – now, along a green
motorway, make a beeline for
Weobley, guided by its church spire,
the second tallest in the county.

At a kissing gate go straight
through, over the ring and bailey.
Another gate and you are at the top
of the main street.

The village's name probably derives
from 'Wibba's Ley', a ley being a
woodland glade and the land
belonging to a man with that Saxon
name. It is known that glove-
making and brewing were among
the 7th-century activities in the
village. By the time of Domesday
it was known as Wibelai, later
evolving to Weobley. The village
claims an association with the
famous Hereford cattle. James
Tompkyns (or Tomkins) had
33 children, begot by (only) two
women. Two of these children were
early cattle enthusiasts – they
obviously knew how to breed – but
in truth the Herefords that we know
today were not bred in a controlled
way until well into the 18th century.
In spite of this connection with
cattle, conspicuous in its absence
from Weobley today is any visible
market place. The isosceles triangle
at the top of the village, now
occupied by a rose garden and bus
shelter, marks the spot. The market
hall was demolished in the mid-
19th century, whereas a fire –
probably started in a basement
bakery – destroyed the adjoining
row of 15th- to 17th-century houses
in November 1943.

To return to the car park, go
straight down the main street, then
turn left at **The Old Corner House**.

Walk 46

Cats and Dogs on the Black Hill

Visit the highest point in the two counties, where the harsh life has been portrayed in an absorbing novel.

•DISTANCE•	8¾ miles (14.1km)
•MINIMUM TIME•	4hrs
•ASCENT / GRADIENT•	1,475ft (450m) ▲▲▲
•LEVEL OF DIFFICULTY•	🚶 🚶 🚶
•PATHS•	Muddy patches, stony descent, lanes, minor roads, 7 stiles
•LANDSCAPE•	Mountainous plateau incised by green valleys
•SUGGESTED MAP•	aqua3 OS Explorer OL13 Brecon Beacons (East)
•START / FINISH•	Grid reference: SO 288328
•DOG FRIENDLINESS•	A good yomp, but may be sheep grazing on tops
•PARKING•	Black Hill car park (signposted)
•PUBLIC TOILETS•	None on route

BACKGROUND TO THE WALK

Tucked away on the western edge of Herefordshire are three valleys: the River Dore in the Golden Valley, the Escley Brook in the Escley Valley and lastly the Olchon Brook in the Olchon Valley. The Black Hill lies, sometimes literally, in the shadow of the Black Mountains that here delineate the Welsh border.

High Start

Even at the car park – almost 1,300ft (396m) – you are higher than most tops attained elsewhere in this book. Known locally as 'the Cat's Back', Black Hill distinguishes itself by being the highest peak in Herefordshire (and in Worcestershire) that the Ordnance Survey names on its maps. The Ordnance Survey gives no such attention to the actual highest point in Herefordshire, a knuckle on one of the Black Mountains' splayed-out fingers, lying as it does along the boundary with Wales – so let's call that 'the Dog's Back'. In fine, summertime weather you cannot fail to enjoy this airy walk, but should you do it in cold and wet conditions, you will need a heart of stone not to empathise with those upland farmers who have no choice but to be working outdoors in such conditions.

Realistic Fiction

Bruce Chatwin's 1983 book *On the Black Hill* was largely biographical, tracing the history of the Jones family through some 70 years of farming on the Black Hill. He had spent much time in the Herefordshire borders and had befriended several people. At first it may seem odd that a book about outdoor, farming people should be claustrophobic, but it is a short distance from solitude to isolation, and even in the 21st century people who work on the land are often in solitude for protracted periods of time. In the case of the novel's Jones brothers, Benjamin and Lewis, they are emotionally intense, largely because they have so few relationships and because of their blood ties. (In the film of the same name, directed by Andrew Grieve and released in 1988, the actors playing the brothers were real brothers too.)

Bruce Chatwin's *On the Black Hill* was his first novel. He had arrived at writing by a roundabout route, first as an auctioneer and later as head of one of London's famous auction houses, then as an archaeologist. His diverse career was typical of his life; he attributed his adaptability and somewhat 'nomadic' lifestyle to his wartime childhood, during which he was cared for by various aunts in various places. He went on to write several other novels, realising his goal of not being a formula writer but making each book quite different to any that preceded it, although many people find them 'inaccessible'.

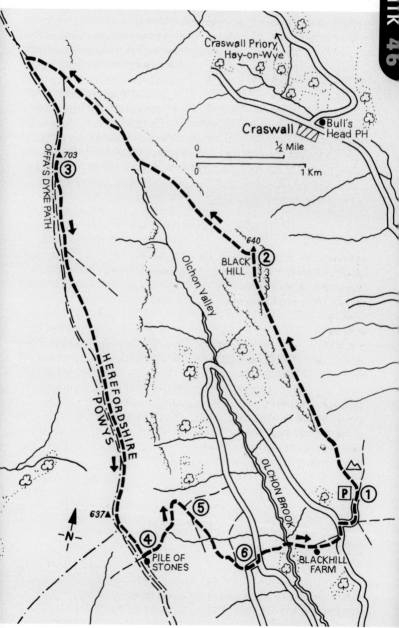

Walk 46 Directions

① From the car park go straight and steeply up the clear track. Just keep going, enjoying the airy path, or, if the wind is strong, walk in the lee on the eastern side when the terrain permits. The gradient varies over the 1½ miles (2.4km) to the trig point.

WHERE TO EAT AND DRINK   ⓘ

In Craswall, the menu at the **Bull's Head** free house includes pan-fried hake, Craswall pie and Olchon lamb. Dogs welcome. In Michaelchurch Escley the **Bridge Inn**, adjacent to the Escley Brook and a tiny camping site, offers home-cooked food using local produce such as Herefordshire beef and salmon smoked in Hereford city. It has a brookside beer garden. Dogs and children are welcome.

---

② Continue along what is now an easy, broad ridge for 1¾ miles (2.8km), to a low, concrete slab. Turn left here, joining both **Offa's Dyke Path** and the border between England and Wales. In a little over ½ mile (800m) is a very indistinct top – at 2,305ft (703m), the highest point of all the walks in this book.

③ Now carry on for 2½ miles (4km) along this gorgeous ridge: the point where you turn off is indicated by a pile of stones and a similar concrete slab indicating Offa's Dyke Path again – this point is approximately perpendicular to the sharp end of

Black Hill. You may be able to see your car from here, and the re-ascent necessary to return to it.

④ Turn left. The descent begins with a left-hand traverse. After 650yds (594m) be sure to swing round to the right, heading down the valley. When 140yds (128m) beyond this sharp bend, note, but do not take, a waymarker indicating a left turn option (in late summer the waymarker may be concealed by bracken). After 30yds (27m) come to a very finely forked junction.

⑤ Be sure to take the lower, left-hand option; do not go 'straight on', that is, the right fork. Descend to a gate and the first stile of the day. Walk along a sunken track to a second stile. Turn left down an old sunken lane. Later ignore a stile on the left and reach a minor road.

⑥ Descend to a junction. Turn left. Within 60yds (55m) take a footpath on the right, down into trees to cross the **Olchon Brook**, then re-ascend. Go round buildings at **Blackhill Farm** and continue up through small fields to the road you came in on. Turn left then right to return to your car.

WHAT TO LOOK FOR   ⓘ

Look out for energetic **Offa's Dyke Path walkers**. They started in Chepstow and so are only a couple of days into the walk. Those who started in the north are probably tiring, so won't overtake you!

WHILE YOU'RE THERE   ⓘ

A few miles along the road to Hay-on-Wye, not signposted and tucked out of sight in a valley, are the forlorn remains of **Craswall Priory**. Even in this corner of Herefordshire, remoteness is a relative concept – this building just doesn't get visited by the numbers associated with Dore Abbey (► Walk 41) or Longtown Castle (► Walk 50). Craswall is the third and final Grandmontine priory in England, the others being in Grosmont, North Yorkshire and Alderbury, Wiltshire. The priory was probably built in the 1220s, and abandoned in 1441. It is a Listed Grade II, Scheduled Ancient Monument.

Shrunken Clifford – an Original Settlement

A circuit of a 'backwater' of the River Wye, visiting a village with a significant history.

•DISTANCE•	5½ miles (8.8km)
•MINIMUM TIME•	2hrs 30min
•ASCENT / GRADIENT•	560ft (171m) ▲▲▲
•LEVEL OF DIFFICULTY•	🚶🚶 🚶🚶 🚶🚶
•PATHS•	Field paths and lanes, awkward embankment, over 30 stiles
•LANDSCAPE•	Rolling hills and Wye Valley views
•SUGGESTED MAP•	aqua3 OS Explorer 201 Knighton & Presteigne
•START / FINISH•	Grid reference: SO 251450
•DOG FRIENDLINESS•	Lots of stiles; lots of cows, sheep and horses
•PARKING•	Roadside parking at St Mary's Church, Llanfair
•PUBLIC TOILETS•	None on route

BACKGROUND TO THE WALK

Clifford itself was a planned Norman town of perhaps 200 dwellings. The parish appears as Cliford in the 1086 Domesday survey, and maps of Herefordshire dating from the 1360s show only three significant settlements – Hereford itself, Wigmore and Clifford. We know that William Fitz Osborn (later the 1st Earl of Hereford) had a castle built on the site in about 1070, having been given the ground by William the Conqueror.

Defensive Flooding

Apart from the natural defences afforded by the spur of land beside the river (the name deriving from a modest cliff near where the river was fordable), an earth dam has been identified on the western, upstream side of the castle. This would have enhanced the castle's defences by creating a considerable lake – it's a natural flood plain, as the absence of contours on the map shows. What you see today – which isn't much – was built in about 1250, but the earthworks are substantial. The castle is privately owned (sold in 2002), so you have to peep in from the road. As one of several Welsh border defences, it has at times been a focus of war, suffering particularly in the 16th century. As for the vanished parts of the castle, doubtless the stone was put to good use – it is said that both Upper Court and Lower Court in the village are built of it.

Llanfair

A contemporary building that has escaped the ravages of war and withstood the ravages of time is St Mary's Church. The church is actually at Llanfair, in a 'Red Riding Hood' setting, a good ½ mile (800m) uphill from the castle; the reason for this separation is not completely clear – perhaps it was literally to distance it from conflict? Much of the present-day church is Victorian. Among its features are four family shields on the belfry roof and a rare 13th-century wooden effigy, which bears a striking resemblance to the one in Hereford Cathedral of Bishop Aquablanca. Priory Farm is so-called because it was built on the site of the priory of Cluniac monks, founded in about 1130, and named after a religious order originating in Cluny in France some 200 years earlier. The adjacent fish ponds, presumably dug out by the monks, would have provided their community with a valuable source of protein. On the route you'll cross and re-cross the dismantled railway that connected Dorstone, in the heart of the Golden Valley, with Hay-on-Wye. It joined the line that served Hereford and Hay (and on to Brecon) about a mile (1.6km) south west of Clifford, the line from Hereford having been built 25 years earlier, in 1864.

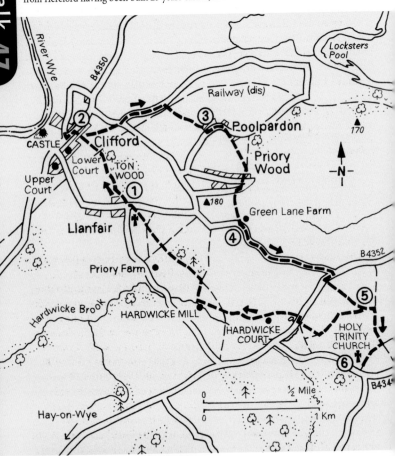

Walk 47 Directions

① A few paces past the road junction at the corner of the churchyard, take some wooden steps on the right. Yellow arrows indicate your route. Leave **Ton Wood** by a gate on the left, beside a wire game-breeding enclosure. More arrows lead across the old

railway towards **Clifford**. Leave the last meadow beside a house, noting the two arrows for those coming from Clifford.

② Walk to the road. Turn left then right for the **castle**. Retrace your steps to Point ②. Now take the arrow pointing to a row of oaks. At the tarmac beyond follow 'Unsuitable for heavy goods vehicles'. On the right, after 440yds (402m) search for a stile up steep steps. It's probably hidden by elder and hawthorn (and bracken) – easier is a small metal gate 30yds (27m) before the stile. Across this green strip scramble down and up the railway embankment again. Halfway up the field switch the hedge from your left to your right. Find a stile behind a derelict yellow-and-red harvester. A wooded path soon reaches a lane.

WHILE YOU'RE THERE ⓘ

For many, a visit to the Golden Valley is incomplete without a stop in **Hay-on-Wye**. Even if you are not a hoarder of books – Hay is famous for its second-hand and specialist bookshops – time is easily spent wandering about in this sporadically vibrant town. For something serene and different, try paddling a very stable canoe down the Wye – **Celtic Canoes** and **Paddles and Pedals** are both in Hay.

---

③ Turn left. In 230yds (210m), before rusty sheds, strike right, to a stile behind six hawthorns in a dip. Through a garden, take the rough track joining two tarmac lanes. Turn right for perhaps 30 paces. A waymarker points towards a stile in trees. Go straight down this field to meet a lane.

④ Turn left along the lane. Stride out for ½ mile (800m) to reach the **B4352**. Turn right. In 70yds (64m)

WHERE TO EAT AND DRINK ⓘ

Clifford lost its pub – the Clifford Castle Inn – decades ago. About 1¾ miles (2.8km) north east of Hardwicke, along the B4352, you'll find the **Castlefield Inn** for bar meals and real ales. It has a children's play area. Otherwise head west for an abundance of options in **Hay-on-Wye** – a spin-off from its fame.

WHAT TO LOOK FOR ⓘ

Besides its lush cattle-grazed meadows and orchards, Herefordshire is important for potatoes. Consequently **ridge-and-furrow patterns** have been mostly lost to the deep workings of the modern plough. However, a fine example is in the pasture from Poolpardon up to Priory Wood. Hardwicke's **Holy Trinity Church** is a picture in sunlight. This 14th-century style structure was only built in 1851.

---

cross to a stile. In this vast meadow aim to the right of trees on the skyline, then the stile by a white-walled house.

⑤ Pass through the garden. Take the bridleway, right. After a leafy interlude join a stony track, but within 160yds (146m), where a footpath crosses, turn right, to reach **Holy Trinity Church** easily.

⑥ Retrace your steps to Point ⑤. Go diagonally left to a stile completely hidden by a protruding hedge. Turn right, around two sides of this field. In the next one turn right, along the field edge. Take the driveway near by. At **Hardwicke Court** step around a wall to walk right beside the building, down a flagstone path on a manicured lawn. At the bottom, through a small gate, maintain this line, although the 'Road Used as a Public Path' is obliterated. At a farm gate go straight ahead, past a gigantic oak, to find a wicket gate – the 'RUPP' becomes more defined. Do not take the waymarked stile 40yds (37m) to the right. At **Hardwicke Mill** go into the garden. Leave by a stile on the right. Ascend this field edge, striking left at the trees. Having skirted to the right of a house, you'll see St Mary's Church across fields ahead. Head for the church and the start of the walk.

Rent-a-Bee in the Golden Valley

A busy pilgrimage from the River Dore to the River Wye and back, across a heavenly landscape.

•DISTANCE•	6 miles (9.7km)
•MINIMUM TIME•	3hrs
•ASCENT / GRADIENT•	1,165ft (355m) ▲ ▲ ▲
•LEVEL OF DIFFICULTY•	👬 👬 👬
•PATHS•	Minor lanes, good tracks, meadows, couple of short but severe descents over grass, 24 stiles
•LANDSCAPE•	A route with many picnic opportunities!
•SUGGESTED MAP•	aqua3 OS Explorer 201 Knighton & Presteigne or OL13 Brecon Beacons (East)
•START / FINISH•	Grid reference: SO 313416
•DOG FRIENDLINESS•	Grazing land, but some freedom in sections of woodland
•PARKING•	Car park beside Dorstone Post Office
•PUBLIC TOILETS•	Beside village hall, near green

BACKGROUND TO THE WALK

Bees are fascinating. One could write a book this size just on the biology and sociology of bees, and still have much to write. We shall have to content ourselves with a little bit about how Herefordshire has benefited from them. Beekeeping is a combination of science, art and skilled labour, an all-consuming hobby or, occasionally, a way of earning a living. After Dorstone, the next village going south is Peterchurch, home of Golden Valley Apiaries and where David Williams and his father before him have kept bees since 1959.

Contract Pollinators

At one time David and June Williams' Golden Valley Apiaries managed over 540 colonies of bees, although today the number is closer to 100. A typical year would yield 8½–10 tonnes of honey – about 20,000 1lb jars – but one exceptionally good year produced over 13 tonnes. The honey, which has won prizes at the Three Counties Show and the Royal Welsh Show, is largely sold through local shops, with some being sold in bulk to packing companies. (A meagre 5 per cent of the 25,000 tonnes of honey eaten in the UK each year is produced by British bees – so much for food mountains.)

All this honey has to be collected. Bees typically forage over a distance of about 1½ miles (2.4km). Fruit growing is financially a high-risk venture – apples and pears, but more so the soft fruits such as blackcurrants, raspberries and strawberries – so rather than leave pollination to chance, growers hire colonies of bees. Although almost impossible to measure scientifically, it is generally reckoned that hiring bees during the flowering period can improve the fruit yield by 30–40 per cent compared with merely relying on the local, wild bee population.

Most of Golden Valleys Apiaries' work is within a 40-mile (64km) radius. Bees are early risers – to deliver bees to a site means getting the hives into a vehicle before first light –

otherwise, particularly on warmer mornings, the bees may have taken flight. Typically the hives are kept on a site for four to six weeks. Bees don't like the rain, but yields of honey are only seriously affected if there is very protracted wet weather. The greatest danger to the flowers they are pollinating is a late frost, but the fruits themselves are also susceptible to adverse weather such as heavy downpours and freakish hailstorms at picking time.

Any species is susceptible to diseases and viruses. Over 100 colonies were lost in the Golden Valley when varroasis struck in 1994–5. The crab-like mite *Varroa jacobsoni* is a mere 0.04 inches (1.1mm) long and 0.11 inches (1.7mm) wide. It is a parasite, sucking blood from the bee. In addition, the mite lays eggs in the honeycomb; once hatched, these suck blood through the body wall of the pupa of the honey bee. The colony will almost certainly be lost as the mites are often found only when it is too late.

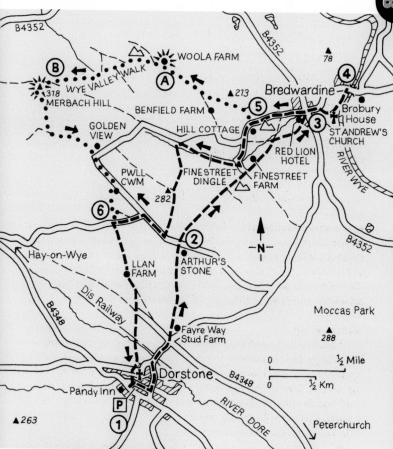

Walk 48 Directions

① Go down the near side of the triangular village green but turn right (not to the church), passing fine houses with finer views. At the

lane end turn left, passing D'Or Produce Ltd (who pack potatoes). At the **B4348** care is required. Go straight ahead, bridging the **River Dore**. Be sure to switch sides before the road bends severely right. Follow the driveway towards **Fayre**

Walk 48

WHILE YOU'RE THERE ⓘ

St Andrew's Church at Bredwardine is very much Kilvert's church, being where the Victorian diarist was rector when he died of peritonitis in 1879. It has a huge 12th-century font. **Brobury House Gardens** – seen from Point ④ – extend to 5 acres (2ha) in formal Victorian style.

Way Stud Farm. A clearly waymarked route across pastures leads directly up to **Arthur's Stone**.

② Beyond Arthur's Stone take a fingerpost. Cross the second field diagonally. Follow the left side of an ineffective fence to a stile left of the corner. Two fields further descend very steeply on grass beside larches. Keep beside the hedge to find an awkward stile. Take the lane but skirt right of **Finestreet Farm** using several stiles. In another steep meadow find a stile below and left of a massive standing oak with a fallen one beside it. Cross a field diagonally, to pass beside a newly renovated, timber-framed house. Beyond is **Bredwardine**.

③ Cross the road carefully. In 80yds (73m) an avenue leads to **St Andrew's Church**. At the very end a stile and waymarkers lead to Bredwardine's bridge over the River Wye – ideal for a picnic.

④ Go back to Point ③. Take the '25%' gradient road beside the **Red Lion Hotel**. Go 700yds (640m) up this lane, including its steepest section, to just before **Hill Cottage**: here a fingerpost points right, and behind you is a '1 in 4' sign. (Here Walk 49 goes right.)

⑤ Keep ahead, ignoring a right turn after 160yds (146m). When the road rises sharply after a stream, find a gate on the right, just past a

house (called Finestreet Dingle). Now ascend this dell (also called **Finestreet Dingle**) guided by blue arrows. In front of a house turn left then left again, to skirt a plantation. A row of hawthorns points to your stile near the brow. Tackle an awkward gate near some scrawny pines, keeping this line to a minor road. Turn right. In 325yds (297m) turn left (sign '20%'). Down here after another 325yds (297m) find a fingerpost, hidden behind a holly tree. (Walk 49 rejoins here.)

WHERE TO EAT AND DRINK ⓘ

Dorstone's **Pandy Inn** sits serenely overlooking the village green. It has a delightful beer garden and play equipment for children. Its food has won many plaudits – best to eat after your walk, otherwise you may simply get too comfortable. Roughly half-way round, in Bredwardine, the handsome **Red Lion Hotel** is an irresistibly convenient place to stop, particularly as you'll pass it twice.

⑥ Soon join the track visible ahead. Now rattle on, to and through **Llan Farm**. However, 220yds (201m) beyond it, take the diagonal footpath (not the old lane, right). Cross a sunken lane, the old railway, then the village playing fields to reach the road near the church. Cross over, then skirt right of the churchyard, along a fenced path, to the village green and the start.

WHAT TO LOOK FOR ⓘ

Look out for **wind farms**. One is planned for Vagar Hill, plumb in line with Hay Bluff when viewed from Arthur's Stone. It is to help meet 'renewable energy targets'. In autumn 2002 over 250 people, many belonging to Friends of the Golden Valley, attended a meeting at which the plans were presented … this story could run and run. **Arthur's Stone** itself is a chambered tomb dated 3700–2700 BC.

A Climb on to Marvellous Merbach Hill

It's worth the climb to attain the high spot dividing the valleys of the River Dore and the River Wye.

See map and information panel for Walk 48

•DISTANCE•	7 miles (11.3km)
•MINIMUM TIME•	3hrs 30min
•ASCENT / GRADIENT•	1,330ft (405m) ▲▲▲
•LEVEL OF DIFFICULTY•	👫 👫 👫

Walk 49 Directions (Walk 48 option)

Turn right at Point ⑤ on Walk 48. In perhaps 100yds (91m), where the drive bends, take a gate with a blue 'Wye Valley Walk' marker. Follow the field boundary on your left, initially staying low. Through a triply fastened gate, gradually ease away from the field boundary, ascending. Join the track from **Benfield Farm** at a cattle grid and a green-on-white sign, 'Woola'.

Now seemingly in forest, walk for 400yds (366m), to between the penultimate and final pole before the farm, Point Ⓐ. A wooden handrail marks some steps to a path that skirts **Woola Farm**. What price its view? Join a steep, extensively cracked concrete track, uphill.

Pass to the right of some corrugated sheds just before the brow of the hill. This is something of a false top, but the way to Merbach Hill is clear ahead. In the last field before the common, hug the field boundary on the left to observe the right of way, then, over the stile, turn right for 40yds (37m) to resume your line. A green path cuts through scattered hawthorn, silver birch and rowan in what in summer is a sea of otherwise impenetrable bracken and brambles. You will come to a clear fork, Point Ⓑ, where the Wye Valley Walk veers slightly right on a level track. Take the left fork, for here you are just 130yds (119m) from a memorable view. Whatever the origin of the Golden Valley's name may be, when you are atop **Merbach Hill** you cannot refute that you have struck a rich vein of scenery.

Prominent to the south west is Hay Bluff: head towards it for about 60yds (55m), to reach a good path. Turn left, to an easily seen wicket gate. Enjoy this modest, sheep-grazed plateau to pick up a dirt track from **Golden View**. Go ahead on the tarmac lane for 350yds (320m), taking a fingerpost just before **Pwll Cwm**. Go down the left edge of two fields. Turn left on a gravelly, grassy lane for 50yds (46m). Now take a stile on the right. Out of this field, take a few paces to your left, rejoining Walk 48 at a fingerpost and a holly tree, Point ⑥.

The Lower Olchon Valley

Walking way-out west, where the times are scarcely a-changing.

•**DISTANCE**•	5¼ miles (8.4km)
•**MINIMUM TIME**•	2hrs 45min
•**ASCENT / GRADIENT**•	655ft (200m) ▲▲▲
•**LEVEL OF DIFFICULTY**•	🚶🚶 🚶🚶 🚶🚶
•**PATHS**•	Lanes, tracks and field paths in mixed farmland, 18 stiles
•**LANDSCAPE**•	Rolling farmland and the Black Mountains ridge
•**SUGGESTED MAP**•	aqua3 OS Explorer OL13 Brecon Beacons (East)
•**START / FINISH**•	Grid reference: SO 324287
•**DOG FRIENDLINESS**•	Under close control; small dogs may need help on stiles
•**PARKING**•	About 300yds (274m) north of Crown Inn, Longtown, on castle road, in long bay beside row of large, new houses
•**PUBLIC TOILETS**•	None on route

Walk 50 Directions

Take a path behind the telephone box. Go diagonally right to reach a road bridge. Turn left then right. Soon after crossing the **Escley Brook** turn left beside a driveway. Walk to the far right-hand corner of this field, curving right to a gate. In 75yds (69m) ignore the lower field and follow the waymarked route, with the hedge on your left. Cross a rivulet by a three-plank bridge, the Escley Brook now on your left. After stepping stones walk through woodland. Leave by wooden steps, then a stile. Go slightly right to a gate. Continue, roughly level with a young hedgerow on your left.

Throughout Herefordshire, Environmental Improvement Grants are available. The scheme is entirely funded by the Herefordshire Council. Applications may be made by small landowners, individuals, parish councils and community groups. For work to be finished by February 2003 the maximum grant available was £500. Grants are available not only for the planting of hedgerows but also for laying already established hedges, planting or pruning fruit trees for orchards, and fencing associated with any of the planting activities.

Through a small metal gate, dip down for some 30yds (27m) to turn right, joining a track. Soon take a gate into woodland, signposted 'Countryside Access Scheme' – ignore the yellow waymarked route down to the left. Instead, a footbridge leads you into a small conifer plantation. In 125yds (114m) turn right. At a minor road turn right. At the T-junction go left for 30yds (27m), then walk up four right-hand field edges; fine views open up.

> ### WHILE YOU'RE THERE ⓘ
> **Longtown Castle** has just enough to fire the imagination, and stunning views. The main part still standing, atop a substantial motte, is the keep. **St Margaret's Church** (between Longtown and Vowchurch on a minor road) has a beautiful rood screen.

By the end of the 1990s average income per head from farming had fallen to just below £10,000. Incomes have risen slightly since then, but 2001's foot and mouth outbreak struck Herefordshire hard. In the county's higher, westernmost hills, almost all farming is livestock farming. One possible vehicle for economic regeneration is the Herefordshire Stone Tile Project. About 7 miles (11.3km) east north east of Longtown is Dore Abbey (► Walk 41). Its stone tile roof is undergoing urgent repair, using stone from nearby quarries or delves. The plan is to reopen other local delves. It will necessitate training local people in the largely forgotten skills of tile dressing. In the case of Dore Abbey, much of the funding is coming from English Heritage. Hopefully this will act as a catalyst to the private home market, for many of the county's private dwellings have stone roofs. In reality, tile dressing might provide a second stream of income for farmers and other agricultural workers, for the shock and strain to the wrists of working the stone would be injurious if carried out full-time.

WHERE TO EAT AND DRINK ⓘ

In Longtown the village **post office shop** (closed on Sundays) has provisions. The **Crown Inn** offers standard fare. Dogs are allowed, as long as they don't chase the cats. In Clodock is the **Cornewall Arms**.

Cross the top field of **Mynydd Merddin**, and one more diagonally, to a hedged and fenced track. Follow this track for less than 150yds (137m), turning right over a stile (with a waymarker). In nearly ½ mile (800m) join the lane just left of **Upper Brooks Farm**. After about 400yds (366m), where this bends left, take the right-hand path

option. Cross one field diagonally. Turn half-right (there should be a hedge on your left-hand side), but in 40yds (37m) take a gate on the left. Move to the right, to walk with the hedge on your right. Descend steadily towards the village of **Clodock**, passing the ruinous buildings of **Garn-galed**. Go straight across the road, beside a house. At the bridge turn left, then immediately right, beside the infant **River Monnow**, soon entering St Clydog's churchyard (hence the name Clodock).

The church is a terrific, largely Norman building. Inside you'll find a three-decker pulpit (a pulpit with a clerk's stall below the vicar's stand and, at the bottom, a reading desk). Also here are three, centuries-old oak chests. The parish's money box had three different locks – the vicar and two of his churchwardens would have held one key each. Don't miss a fascinating stone tablet setting out the Hereford Assizes judgement of 1805 that established monetary payments to be made in lieu of tithe payments, for example, 2d from each household instead of one tenth of its hens' eggs. It's been suggested that the dove – a symbol of peace – carved in one corner of the tablet implies that both sides were happy with the judgement.

After the churchyard cross several meadows, easing away from the water to a tarmac road. Turn right. Soon you reach the recently moved post office and village shop, now in a converted barn at **Tan House Farm**. Here, in season, you will find locally sourced fruit, vegetables and other produce.

Shortly ignore the right fork; your car is ¼ mile (400m) ahead.

Walking in Safety

All these walks are suitable for any reasonably fit person, but less experienced walkers should try the easier walks first. Route finding is usually straightforward, but you will find that an Ordnance Survey map is a useful addition to the route maps and descriptions.

Risks

Although each walk here has been researched with a view to minimising the risks to the walkers who follow its route, no walk in the countryside can be considered to be completely free from risk. Walking in the outdoors will always require a degree of common sense and judgement to ensure that it is as safe as possible.

- Be particularly careful on cliff paths and in upland terrain, where the consequences of a slip can be very serious.

- Remember to check tidal conditions before walking on the seashore.

- Some sections of route are by, or cross, busy roads. Take care and remember traffic is a danger even on minor country lanes.

- Be careful around farmyard machinery and livestock, especially if you have children with you.

- Be aware of the consequences of changes in the weather and check the forecast before you set out. Carry spare clothing and a torch if you are walking in the winter months. Remember the weather can change very quickly at any time of the year, and in moorland and heathland areas, mist and fog can make route finding much harder. D on't set out in these conditions unless you are confident of your navigation skills in poor visibility. In summer remember to take account of the heat and sun; wear a hat and carry spare water.

- On walks away from centres of population you should carry a whistle and survival bag. If you do have an accident requiring the emergency services, make a note of your position as accurately as possible and dial 999.

Acknowledgements

The following information sources were invaluable: Nancy Elliot's *Dore Workhouse in Victorian Times* (1984, Workers' Education Association, Ewyas Harold Branch) for Walk 41, and Gerry Calderbank and Martin Hudson's *Canal, Coal and Tramway* (2000, LC Promotions) for Walk 26. For their help I must also thank: Richard Phillips of Badsey (Walk 5); Professor Jean Emberlin at the National Pollen Research Unit (Walk 18); David Williams of Golden Valley Apiaries (Walk 48); John Coleman, Golden Valley Community Coordinator, and Christine Hope at the new Longtown Post Office (Walk 50). Thank you to Pamela, Eleanor and Fiona for letting me go 'walking working'. This book is dedicated to my Dad, who started me walking.

AQUA3 AA Publishing and Outcrop Publishing Services would like to thank Chartech for supplying aqua3 maps for this book.
For more information visit their website: www.aqua3.com.

Series management: Outcrop Publishing Services Limited, Cumbria
Series editor: Chris Bagshaw **Copy editor:** Jenni Davis
Front cover: www.BritainonView.com **Back cover:** AA Photo Library/J Martin